Get Your Child Ready for Kindergarten (and Start Early)

Get Your Child Ready for Kindergarten (and Start Early)

A KINDERGARTEN TEACHER EXPLAINS WHAT TO EXPECT AND HOW TO PREPARE

Jennifer Minogue, M.Ed.

For Johnny, Brooke, and Sarah-
I love you.

For all my past and present students-
I have loved being your teacher.

TABLE OF CONTENTS

CHAPTER 1

Preparation is Key

A ll we ever needed to know in life we learned in kindergarten. Have you ever heard that expression? What if I told you that the preparation for life started well before kindergarten?!

For 25 years I have been a public elementary school teacher in an area known for excellence in education. For many of those years I have been fortunate enough to teach kindergarten. During this time, I have taught hundreds of children and have amassed knowledge and insight about the foundational skills students need to be prepared for kindergarten. Every fall, kindergarten teachers everywhere meet new students who are just 4 or 5 years of age. The difference in background knowledge from one 5-year-old child to another can be substantial. A few short years of preparation, or lack thereof, can make such a difference in terms of a child's learning. A little preparation can go a long way in any area of life. Why not help your child off to the best start possible in their educational life? Preparation breeds confidence, and confidence breeds success, even in kindergarten.

Year after year, parents everywhere are surprised to find how academic kindergarten has become. They find out a little too late that their children could have benefited greatly from some advance preparation in certain fundamental academic and social areas. Year after year, teachers everywhere meet with parents at parent- teacher conferences and some-times must discuss with parents that their child is already falling behind with learning letters. Parents often do not understand how it is possible that their child could already be behind their peers academically. I wish more parents had access to information prior to entering school. That information could have made a big difference for their child in the early formative years.

Every spring, kindergarten teams across the country screen children who will attend kindergarten the following fall. At these screenings, some children already know their letters, numbers, shapes and how to write their names. When children come in with prior knowledge, teachers often ask students where they learned it. Some children answer that it was learned in "school." Other children answer that their parents taught them.

There are small and inexpensive steps that all parents can take to pre-pare their children for life as a student. As a veteran kindergarten teacher, my desire to share my insights inspired me to write this book for parents. In the following chapters, I will outline some general verbal, social, emo-tional, and academic tips and routines that will help your child on the road to success in school. I hope that I can reach many parents who, in turn, can help their own children become prepared and successful in their milestone kindergarten year.

The kindergarten I knew as a child, and many of us knew as chil-dren, was a day that consisted of a couple of hours of story time, playtime, crafts, and snack. That was the kindergarten of yesteryear. Today, a typical nursery or 3- year- old program looks like what kindergarten used to look like. Kindergarten is the new first grade. Your child will likely be attend-ing a **full day** kindergarten program, as most public and private programs now are.

The main schedule of the kindergarten school day now involves lit-eracy, math, science, social studies, handwriting, and motor activities. I am a proponent of play in kindergarten and am of the belief that there are many benefits of play in kindergarten, which I will address later. But there is a full academic curriculum now and play is just a part. Some schools may incorporate no play at all or limited play.

While kindergarten is technically considered an "early" childhood grade, many public and private school kindergartens are part of the K-12 system. The kindergarten classes are often housed in the elementary school buildings (with grades 1-5). In that setting, the kindergarten will often follow the full day schedule like the older grades do, including lunch in the cafeteria, recess, and weekly visits to special area classes such as art, music, and physical education (more widely known as gym class).

This may all sound daunting but fear not! Kindergarten is where it all begins! It will be an exciting milestone year for your child. Kindergarten is your child's first experience in the big school. It will be a school year filled with new friends, fun projects, and memorable achievements. When we are getting our children ready for kindergarten, we need to consider the whole child: academic, social, and emotional.

Many parents, friends and family members ask me, "What does my child need to know for kindergarten?" That question prompted me to write this book. Parents really want to know how they can help to prepare their children for kindergarten. My answer is too long to convey in a casual conversation. In addition, preparing for kindergarten begins well before kindergarten. Please do not expect or wait for kindergarten to be the place that will teach your children everything they will need to know. Start early with small steps. I have put together ideas from all my years of teaching kindergarten in this book. Get your sticky notes ready to flag any ideas you find useful! My objective is to ensure parents have knowledge about what to expect as your child approaches kindergarten. It comes quicker than you think it will.

CHAPTER 2

Learning Language is Where it all Begins

As an educator, I have always been extremely interested in the process of scaffolding. Scaffolding was one of those buzz words I would hear during my time as an education student. But the term, and what it stands for, has stood the test of time in the circle of educational trends. Scaffolding means exactly what it sounds like: It is when you build knowledge on top of prior knowledge. Many concepts are learned in a scaffolded order. Without a strong foundation in one area, we may be weak in everything we build on top of that. Think of a building. If the foundation is not strong, if there are gaps in the bottom tier, everything above that has the potential to be faulty or crumble.

Foundations are extremely important in the early years of learning too. Babies do not learn to run before they crawl. Likewise, children will not learn to read well if they do not have solid foundations in language, meaning, and sounds. Scaffolding new knowledge on top of prior knowledge is key.

Preparing your child for life as a student begins years before your child becomes a student. It starts when your child is born. That is when the learning begins! It starts with the understanding of language. Exposure to conversation is one super easy way to help your child learn basic language skills. Through listening, children learn that dialogue, or conversation, is a way to communicate and to ask for what we need. Conversation is free and is a great way to get your child learning language. Talk, talk, talk. Children are great company! When you are a parent of a young child, it is hard to view it that way because we are so busy and in the trenches of it all, but it is the truth.

When I was 14, my baby brother was born. Because of my age I was able to help my mother, witness first-hand what childcare involved, and learn from it. I learned a lot about how to take care of a baby (knowledge I would remember and be grateful for years later when I became a mom myself).

I remember my mother speaking endlessly to my baby brother, telling him stories, narrating her actions for him when he was just an infant. She explained to me that he would learn language and how to speak through exposure to words, and that the more we spoke in front of him and immersed him in language, the more language he would learn. This was very interesting to me. Coincidence or not, he was a very smart child with good language skills. My brother spoke very early. By the age of three, he was having fluid conversations with adults and had much background information about various subjects. I became a believer in what my mother had explained to me, that simply engaging your baby in conversation helps them acquire language.

You may be thinking *that is just common sense that a child would learn language by being immersed in it.* Yes, it is common sense. It seems so easy that it should go without saying, right? Wrong. I have heard parents say they do not talk to their baby because their baby cannot talk yet. My argument is, then how will the baby learn to talk? From whom will the baby learn language? Children learn language by having it modeled for them. I cannot stress it enough! Talk to your baby or toddler! Point out objects, call them by name. Narrate your actions. When you go for a walk, point out what you are seeing along the way. "Do you see the tree? What color are the leaves? The leaves are green." If you are reading this then I will assume you have a child who is headed to kindergarten at some point soon. If your child is past the baby stage, do not worry. Start conversing with your child now. Each day is a new day to improve as a parent and learn. Parenting is a process. Through it we learn about ourselves and grow. As humans, we are a work in progress. As parents, we want what is best for our children and each day is an opportunity to get better. I firmly believe that.

Take advantage of every teaching moment. It will pay dividends in your child's development of language and words. I say turn off the electronics and the television and enjoy educational time at home. Devices will not teach your child to pay attention. In fact, I believe that using the devices at too early of an age has disadvantages and takes time away from authentic learning time. Electronics seem to overstimulate very small preschool age children, from what I have seen. Many children have difficulty sitting and focusing for a stretch of time, but in front of a computer, laptop, or television the same kids can sit still for long lengths. Children are seemingly trained to do this by overuse of electronics. Electronics cannot take the place of real communication, and for that reason I would suggest placing age appropriate time limits on any screen time.

Go for walks. Go to the playground. Go to the public library and take advantage of their free programs, toy room, blocks, story time, crafts, and whatever other programs they offer. When my daughters were babies, we spent a lot of time at the library at the Mommy and me programs. The other great benefit of going to your local library for programs is that the programs at the library for that age group will have other parents from your area with children the same age. My daughter met other children there who were kids she would be going to kindergarten with. As a matter of fact, the girl who was her best friend in pre-k was a child she met at the library in a Mommy and me class. I became friendly with the mom, and we had a lot in common. She had two daughters the same age as my daughters, and we sometimes would meet at the playground or museum. When my older daughter went to school, she already had a friend.

Explain to your little one how and why you do things such as water plants, make lunch, wash, and fold clothes. Your child is a little person. Little ones are good company! Enjoy your time with them while they are little. Talk about the weather. Discuss the sounds you hear as you walk outside: birds, cars, insects- whatever you may see and hear, weave it into the conversation. Read road signs. Sing silly songs in the car. Speak to and with your child. Do it often.

Even in the infant stage, your job as your child's first teacher has begun. Do not underestimate the importance of that job or the long-term cause and effect nature of your actions as a parent in the early years. Begin to narrate your actions and it will teach vocabulary.

Many of us are very busy and/or we are working parents. We work all day and we may have child care. When we get home there is dinner to make and laundry to do. There are bills to pay, calls to make, and the list goes on. I understand all of this and I live it too.

Despite all the noise in your life, prioritize your children. Carve out whatever time you can for your children. I think spending time with your children is an activity that pays dividends for a lifetime. The time you spend with your children is a true investment in their future and in your own. Children grow very fast. Before long, they are not children anymore at all! Your kids will grow up better for having spent quality time with family. The infant stage is a time for talking to your baby. Keep the atmosphere calm! Baby is also learning about emotions. Your baby will absorb the environment around them.

We cannot just say, "Do as I say, not as I do." Parenting is modeling. You are modeling the behavior that your child will learn, for better or for worse. Please realize the power in that. Be responsible with it. Children feel "all the feels."

Along these lines, I like to believe that my classroom atmosphere is part of the curriculum. I try to create an atmosphere of positivity that will radiate. I remind myself that I am the one setting the tone and atmosphere in the classroom, not the other way around. I take that responsibility seriously and like to have a classroom atmosphere that is organized, calm, kind, and conducive to learning and socializing all at the same time.

I believe we can also relate that to the role of a parent at home in a child's life. Your home atmosphere is part of your curriculum. What are your own words, actions, and emotions teaching your child? How do the people in your home communicate with one another and what is that teaching your child? How do you respond to different situations? What lessons is that teaching your child? Your child is learning all of that and absorbing it. Your child is learning that the way you communicate is the correct way for your child to communicate. What kind of language and tone are you using? Is it kind? Is it polite? Is it respectful? Are you modeling the way you want your child to also communicate? Are you modeling the way you want your child to handle their own situations?

Apples come from apples. I remember being on the playground with my own children a long time ago. We had a park nearby and would walk there after dinner each night. There was a family who was sometimes there at the same time as us. I sometimes would hear a little tiny voice say a curse word on the playground. I would look around and it was this angelic little toddler using these words.

Looking around, it seemed other children were unphased by the word, which I gathered meant either they had never heard the word before, or had heard it so frequently that they paid no attention to it. In any case, no one knew yet that it was a word not to use, or so it seemed. It was apparent this was language the child learned from hearing it used. While she would not be allowed to use the word in school, she did not know that yet because to her, it was perfectly normal. I was wondering what would happen the first time she went to school and unknowingly said it. This story is just a funny anecdote, but the lesson is if you do not want your children to curse on the first day of kindergarten, you would want to limit the cursing in front of them at home!

If you want a peaceful atmosphere for your child, create it. Babies need to sleep well, eat well, exercise, absorb love, and have peace. It is all basic. Create the beautiful and warm home that you want for your child. I do not mean the look and the aesthetic and the materialness of it. I mean the atmosphere. Speak to your child, play calm music, socialize your child with family and friends, be a protector, and give your child security.

CHAPTER 3

Helping Your Child Learn Language During the Nursery/Toddler Stage

There are simple ways to help your child learn language. I love puzzles. I absolutely love them. I use them in my classroom in literacy centers at the beginning of the school year. Puzzles teach problem solving in a fun way. Puzzles feel like a game but they are learning in disguise. Puzzles have a second benefit when you do an uppercase/lowercase letter match, or one that matches the beginning sound to a word, or even one that matches a baby animal with its mother. Puzzles like this are so effortless and easy to do with your child, and are relatively inexpensive. When your child is little, puzzles can be given as a gift for a birthday or holiday. Additionally, any time you spend playing with your child is a gift within itself. So instead of watching a television show or movie together for 30 minutes, maybe try a puzzle. For nursery school children there are puzzles that also look like blocks.

At dinner you can play conversation games. You can think of conversation starters as a game. One family member thinks of the topic and each member of the family states their own answer. This is an easy way to teach your child how to think, but also how to speak in a full sentence. For example, if the conversation starter is "My favorite food is…." each person around the table starts with that and finishes the sentence with their own answer. "My favorite food is pizza," etc.

Some other ideas for conversation starters, to name a few, are:

"If I could go anywhere, I would go to…"

"My favorite animal is … because…"

"I think the best weather to play outside is…"

"My favorite sport is…"

"My favorite book is…"

You can think of a thousand story starters just like this. Playing a game at dinner might distract children who do not want to eat their veggies or who fight with their siblings. It might just add an element of fun at the end of a stressful day, who knows? It is worth a try. This can also be played in the car.

If you play this game, you may see your children coming up with their own conversation starters. With small children you can play this game to build language and vocabulary and the children love it! It is also a great way to learn information about one another.

Another conversation game you can play with your children is a guessing game. I remember loving this game when I was a little girl. My family would play this game sometimes when we were waiting for food at a restaurant or driving in the car. The game goes like this: One person thinks of an item but does not give any clues as to what it is. Each other person must ask a question that can only be answered with a "yes" or a "no." The questions keep going and going until someone guesses the item. The winner becomes the next person to think of an item. And so on. I love this game for kids because it teaches children how to ask good questions in a fun way. You only get to ask one question during each turn, so you must be wise about what question you ask.

At age 3 or so, I began to introduce my children to the letters more formally. When my kids were little, they had small plastic toy animals that had a letter associated with the animal written on it (the alligator had an A, the bear had a B). This is a fun way to introduce letters and begin letter- sound associations. I have found that the associations are an effective, concrete way for teaching letters to start with. Your child may look at the letter A and say "alligator" if that is the picture they are associating with the letter A. That is completely fine and shows that your child is making a connection. There are many letter puzzles available that you can buy or may be able to borrow from a library (again, thinking about what you can do in a cost-effective way to be your child's first teacher). There are some puzzles that match a letter with an animal whose name starts with the same letter. Other puzzles might be an uppercase and lowercase match. The objective is the same. The letters are being introduced and presented in a fun way.

If you have these types of educational games at home, your child is being immersed in the letters. Once your child begins to identify some of the letters, you could introduce the sound each letter makes. Going into kindergarten, many students know letters and some students even know letter sounds. Your nursery school may be and should be doing some activities with letters. In my professional opinion as a kindergarten teacher, a good pre-kindergarten program should most definitely work on letters for kindergarten readiness. I will address that more later on, when I share my advice on what to look for in a pre-k program.

Reading aloud to your child is an important and inexpensive way to teach language to your child. Please, please, please always read books at night with your children. Read to babies also! When you are too tired to think of the words to say, let a good picture book do the talking. Reading with your child in a rocking chair or your favorite big chair is so cozy. We used to have a chenille, big, soft rocker at home that I sat in when I fed my babies bottles. It also served as a cozy read aloud chair for my own children and me. Many wonderful picture books were enjoyed in that big cozy chair.

Many conversations, laughs and hugs happened there. Many unforgettable teaching moments occurred. Many memories were made, memories that did not cost a dime but are priceless. Moments that I cherished then, but cherish even more now as my children are getting older and I want to hold onto their youth. Reading books together provided all this goodness.

You do not need any money to read books. Just go to your local public library and get a library card. Your public library will let you borrow picture books free of charge, just return them every week and take out new ones. Picture books have endless learning opportunities. The discussion is all there for you. The pictures bring the story to life. As you are reading, stop and wonder. Discuss the characters, the setting, and the plot. Make a prediction about what might happen next. Talk about whether you liked the ending. Stopping and thinking about the book is what good readers do. Modeling that will help your child become a thoughtful reader.

You will be absolutely amazed how much your child will begin to love reading if you find great books. As a kindergarten teacher, I give this advice every year to parents. I wish they had known sooner. At the end of this book, you will find a list of some of my favorite titles and authors that my own children and my own kindergarten classes have enjoyed immensely over the years. I have gone through my entire extensive library. The books I have suggested are my personal tried and tested titles that have won the most smiles, laughter, and requests for a second reading!

Take every opportunity to point out print in everyday life. Print awareness is the understanding that print is organized in a certain way. When you show your child a traffic sign, a grocery list, or a menu at a restaurant, you are teaching your child about the meaning of print in everyday life. Print comes in various forms. When it comes time for reading, your children will have less to learn than their peers if they have been exposed to print-rich environments and examples of print. When children "make believe" they are reading, they are showing that they understand a use of print.

Also at the nursery stage, read and sing nursery rhymes! You can find nursery rhymes in the library as well. Rhyming is such an important piece to phonemic awareness (hearing sounds and distinguishing between them), which is integral to reading. Phonemic awareness has shown to be an important predictor of reading skills. When teaching your child rhyming, start first with identifying rhymes. Most children I have taught can identify rhymes before they can produce rhymes. That seems to be the natural succession of learning rhymes. I teach the children that rhyming words are words that have the same ending and sound the same. Give examples. "Bat, cat. Does that rhyme?" Students can give a thumbs up if they think the two words rhyme, and a thumbs down if they think the words do not rhyme.

Once children are comfortable recognizing pairs of rhyming words, you can ask your child to come up with a rhyming word. "Can you think of a word that rhymes with cat?" Please remember that rhyming, like other reading skills, is developmental. It may take some time and then one day it just clicks if you keep at it like we do at school. Sometimes after practicing rhyme for a few months daily, a child will suddenly be able to produce a list of rhyming words. It is so rewarding. My advice would be to keep at it and be patient.

CHAPTER 4

Important Emotional and Social Steps in Early Childhood

Take life slowly. This is hard to do when your children are little. The years seem like a blur. I remember days when my children were babies and I felt like I did not even have enough time to brush my hair or go to the bathroom! I get it. I think all parents go through that.

I look around and I see that many parents have a strong inclination to sign their children up for a million activities. I am sure there are different reasons for doing this. I am sure one of them is maybe getting an hour off to do much needed and important errands. I get it. That time is needed for parents to do what they need to do. However, I would advise you to not *overschedule* your child. Schedule some activities for your child of course. But do not over schedule them. By that I mean do not be busy every second of every day with scheduled activities until it is time to come home and take a bath and go to bed. I see many families who do this. They tell me about how busy they are and sometimes even explain that there is no time for homework or reading books because of sports, art class, play groups, etc. I hear that it all takes up so much time that there is no time to read a book all week. If that is the case, then your child may be too busy, in my mind. Only you can balance your child's schedule just right. Make sure it is indeed a balance.

Quiet time is important. Also important is a child's ability to keep busy and entertain oneself. We cannot realistically provide entertainment for our children all day long. When we stand on our heads to entertain our children, it teaches them that they are the center of the universe. It also teaches them to be reliant on others for activities and entertainment. It also makes any and all down time or quiet time seem like a bummer.

School can be a fun place in its own way. However, as with many things in life, there are times of the day that are less exciting than others. Hence, some children may think it is boring or may go home and tell their parents that school is boring. When your child says school is boring, point out the positives.

Ask your child, "How can it be boring to be around 20 other children the same age and be learning about this new place that has colored tables, a kitchen, blocks, and other fun things?" Try to accentuate the good parts. Maybe some children feel school is not as fun as soccer or whatever activity is planned for after school. Children will adapt and learn that sometimes sitting quietly for a little while is okay, even peaceful.

I think scheduling children with activities is healthy to a point. I think overscheduling children can be counter-productive. I think this point was on display during Covid shut downs. So many children seemed unable to find things to do and were devastated by the loss of their scheduled activities. We learned how to be creative in keeping ourselves busy. Kids were riding bikes and playing outdoors. People were trying to come up with creative, healthy, and positive ways to spend their unscheduled time. Let's not lose that. One positive outcome we can take way from the experience is the ability to keep ourselves occupied.

Yes, of course, parents can and should play with their children. I certainly played a lot with my children when they were little. I think that type of play needs to be on the adult schedule though, and not every time your child asks. Children must learn to be creative on their own, use imagination on their own, and not be entertained all the time. Turn off the devices and limit television. In my opinion, tablets and other devices are not an opportunity to use imagination or communicate in a real way. Your child would be better off to sit with building blocks, dolls, a train set, or even crayons and paper.

Be sure to set aside some quiet time for your little nursery or toddler age child. Bringing your children to a place where they need to be quiet is also good training for school and life (where sometimes you need to be in a place where you need to be quiet!) Life is not a never-ending circus. If you teach your child that it is, your child will be disappointed by reality and may not be able to adjust to the quiet times, one of them being a classroom. There should be time for play and fun, but then also quiet time.

Learning a tiny bit of independence is important for your child at the nursery school age. We can do things for our children and help our children. But what we teach our children to do for themselves helps them even more. Modeling how to do things helps your child more in the long term.

Your child can take baby steps (literally) toward doing some activities independently. Little children love to be helpful and have a sense of responsibility. They love any small job around the house and helping you makes kids feel important and useful! Encourage your child at home to help with such tasks as: getting dressed (including zippers, buttons, snaps), cleaning up their own toys, setting and clearing the table, watering plants, helping feed pets (with supervision), and helping to put away groceries. Little children can also be responsible for helping to make the bed and throwing away their own garbage such as wrappers, juice boxes, etc.

Teaching your child to be a little bit independent starting with small tasks has many benefits for both you and your child. One benefit is that it will help you in the long run by having to do less yourself! If your children can make their own beds, you do not have to do it. If your children can put on their own socks and shoes, you do not have to do it. If your children clean up their own toys, you do not have to do it!!! Are you starting to get the idea? Yes, it is helpful for you to help your children be independent!

Besides being helpful for you, building independence in your child is also building a positive self-image and self-esteem for your child. In my professional experience as a teacher, children who are capable, or perceive themselves as capable, seem to have higher confidence. I would say the same is true for adults. This one is a no brainer for parents. Teach your child some independence with small reasonable tasks like the ones I stated above.

Is this as easily done as it is told? Probably not. What might happen is that when you ask your child to pick up their toys, they may whine and say they do not want to, or escape into another room hoping you didn't notice the mess. This is where positive reinforcement comes in. I will mention it many times. Positive reinforcement is super important in early childhood classrooms and all classrooms. I would add that I believe it is also super important in our job as a parent!

In teaching and psychology courses, we sometimes learn about B.F. Skinner's well-known theories of learning. "Positive reinforcement" is one such theory of B.F. Skinner, that basically means consequences can determine how often a behavior will be repeated. Positive reinforcement, as used in the classroom, is when you reinforce a behavior you want to encourage. It is a way to reward a behavior that you would like your child to repeat and eventually make a habit of. In my years of classroom management, I can tell you that in my opinion, using positive praise and rewarding good behavior work *so much* better than punishing negative behaviors. I will give you a classroom example.

If a teacher is reading a story on the rug and sees two children who are talking and not listening to the story, she has a few choices on how to handle that situation. One choice is to ignore the talking, but that does not produce the result the teacher wants, which is for children to hear and learn from the story. Another choice is to stop the story and tell the two children to stop talking. But in my experience, it is likely the children will go right back to talking.

Finally, and my favorite way to handle this (and also the way that works best) would be for the teacher to stop and look around thoughtfully. Then the teacher should exclaim, "I love the way some children in the class are listening so nicely to the story. Thank you for sitting so nicely and listening."

Like magic, the children who were talking will stop. Without scolding, and without calling negative attention to the children, this way produces the desired result most often, from my experience. Moving positive attention to the children who are doing the correct or desired behavior works better than scolding in my opinion. Children love praise. If someone is being praised for positive behavior, it influences other children to demonstrate the positive behavior as well. This works almost every time. It can work for you at home, too. When your child is doing something positive, point out the good behavior. Praise is a great reward. Everyone likes praise.

Some examples:

"I like the way you tried to zipper your jacket all by yourself!"

"I like the way you shared toys when you played with your sister."

"I like the way you cleaned up your toys!"

"I like the way you washed your hands before you ate."

"I like the way you threw away your own garbage."

"I like the way you spoke in a soft and gentle way to the baby."

"You are getting so good at putting on your own shoes and socks, I am going to let you have extra playtime before bed."

When you are giving praise, be specific about what action you are praising. As you can see, the examples above are more specific than simply saying, "Good job!"

In the classroom, I have found that using specific praise is more effective than using general praise. I still try to use specific praise when I praise my own children. My daughter recently received her year-end grades and her overall average was great. I told her, "I am so proud of you for all the hard work and studying you put in this quarter. You really got good results from that." I want her to know that the good grades were a result of the hard work.

My emphasis is not on how "smart" a child is. Children may view intelligence as being fixed and something that cannot be changed. If we encourage the hard work, and the effort, then the success will come and will seem more attainable, especially for children who do not view themselves as "smart."

Sometimes as a parent or a teacher, it can be hard to find a way to give positive praise when our students or children are testing us. It can be and will be difficult at times for you as a parent to not get frustrated. Children will test us. But they are the children and we are the adults. We are the ones who can control, and should regulate, our emotions and our next words. We are setting an example. So, while it is extremely tempting to show frustration when your own child does not demonstrate the behavior you want, try not to emphasize the negative behaviors. Rather, try praising and rewarding good behavior positively, and see if that works. This method works but it does take time, patience, and consistency. I use positive praise and positive reinforcement as classroom management techniques, and these methods can be used at home too.

CHAPTER 5

Problems on the Playground!

Toddlers and nursery school age children may seem very self-centered by nature. It is not their fault. They simply see the world through their own point of view. It is the only view they know. While it can be challenging, it is important to try and coach your child on working and playing cooperatively with others. Coaching your child through adversities is a key part of parenting and seems to often be overlooked.

When I say coaching, I mean something like what a sports coach does. In sports, the coach's job is to teach the players and then to help correct when the players do not get it right, and then practice some more. Similarly in the classroom, the teacher teaches a concept, then supervises practice and corrects work. In the classroom we emphasize, "I do, we do, you do."

Your child needs similar coaching from their parents throughout childhood (and the teen years as well I will add). When you happen to be lucky enough to witness your child handle a situation in a way that could or should be handled differently, use it as a teaching moment. Teach the desired behavior, and hope your child remembers it the next time. The next time it happens, you may not be there to intervene. Take advantage of those moments as they arise.

I will give you an example. When my daughter was in kindergarten, she was invited along with another girl to a playdate at a friend's house after school for a couple of hours. When the playdate was ending and I arrived to pick her up, the other two mothers were there chatting. The girls were playing, and two of them came in crying. I asked my daughter why she was crying and one of the mothers interrupted, "They can work it out themselves." I silently disagreed with that opinion, and I asked again why the girls were crying. It was something about sharing. I suggested taking turns. The crying stopped and the girls went to give it a try.

A viable solution was offered and accepted by the girls. They were probably happy to have an adult there to help resolve it. And maybe the next time a similar situation arose, they remembered how to handle that. Had I not suggested that the girls share, and had the girls worked it out themselves, it would have been resolved eventually. However, in my experience as an observer of 5-year-old behavior, what likely would have happened was that the more assertive girl in the group, the one who held the most power, would have gotten her way. I have noticed that is usually what happens when children are left to their devices and do not have the tools to work out conflict yet. And then a cycle ensues of a power imbalance among the children, as the fairness has not been taught or demonstrated. A leader would have been established, as from what I have seen, children in a group tend to take on little roles of leaders and followers, not unlike adults. The solution may have worked out in one child's favor, but maybe not fairly for all parties.

The mother who was suggesting that the 5-year-olds work it out for themselves meant well, or maybe wanted to continue her conversation without being interrupted, but I knew the better option was to coach the girls on how to behave when this kind of situation arises. I knew the children did not have the tools or experience to know what the options were for handling the conflict. Someone needed to teach them.

In an early childhood classroom, I believe one of the teacher's roles is to coach in this manner when conflicts arise. I act as a mediator. I model the desired behaviors. I offer the options. I expect the situations to be handled in a kind way. And children learn. Children rise to the occasion when taught and coached to resolve matters in a kind way.

At the end of a recent school year, I was almost brought to tears of joy in my classroom. During center time, some children were sitting at a table doing artwork. The children were having their own little conversation about their artwork. I heard them telling one another, "Good job...I like your coloring...Do you need help with that...Let me show you...That's a good idea."

Every comment I overheard was positive and supportive. At that moment I almost cried and I felt like I had done a good job, as had the children's parents. This is one of the small rewards of teaching that I experience every day. You can experience those rewards as a parent too, during the proud moments when your child shows you that they have learned what you have taught. I believe coaching is a necessary part of parenting. You are not being a "helicopter" when you intervene, teach, and offer fair solutions when small children are arguing or struggling to resolve a conflict. It is the correct and responsible thing to do, in my view.

Playdates and the conflicts that arise from them are teachable moments for parents. I urge you to allow your child to play with friends, as it is a way to learn how to share and resolve conflicts. Be there to help in a fair way. Offer a solution that is fair for all the children involved. You do not need to have playdates at your house to do this. Public playgrounds offer a chance for affordable playdates for children. I make it a point to bring my kindergarten class to the school playground when the weather allows.

Play helps children learn socialization, language, and conflict resolution. I am aware that many children do not have the opportunity for playdates and the school day is their chance to socialize. I look at it as developing the whole child. Your child will also get exercise at the playground and will work on their fine and gross motor skills by running, climbing, and swinging. It is a win-win.

In kindergarten we like to say that sharing is caring. Taking turns is a concept that is very enforced in the nursery, pre-k, and kindergarten years. As mentioned above, turn taking is important when playing. Taking turns is also very important when speaking. Little children love to interrupt, to be the person talking all the time, and to be the center of attention. Parents and grandparents and other family members may think that is super cute at the dinner table and may love it when your little one gets to be the center of attention. The problem comes when your child and 24 other children who are accustomed to being the center of attention come together in a common place, where they all want to be the center of attention and talk at the same time! This scenario is what early childhood teachers everywhere see during the first week of school. To combat the problem, teachers can use a "talking stick," or craft stick with a star on the top. Whoever has the pointer gets to talk. Slowly but surely, we learn to take turns. If your child can do this already, congratulations! If not, politely prompt your child when they interrupt others and kindly say, "Someone else is speaking right now, please wait."

Along with taking turns when speaking goes "being a good listener." Teachers love to say those words! "Are we being good listeners?" I can just hear it being spoken by all the teachers across the world! Good listening is so under-rated, isn't it? Even in adulthood, listening is such an important and sometimes rare life skill! Everyone wants to be heard it seems. In this age of social media and attention getting devices, being a good listener seems a lost art. Let us teach it to our children and restore listening. Part of being a good friend in life is being a good listener.

Being a good listener can also translate into being a good student as well. I realized in college that most of my learning was happening when I really set my mind to what the teacher was saying. So much learning gets lost in the school day, for children of any age, when they are not listening.

If you are not listening in class, you are not learning. This goes for kindergarten, through college, and into your professional life.

In my training to be a teacher we learned about the different ways children learn, and the idea that each person acquires information uniquely and in different ways. Some children are more visual learners and we certainly do have a lot of visual cues in kindergarten. Some children are kinesthetic (hands on learners who learn best by doing) and we have a lot of manipulatives and concrete materials. However, auditory (listening) learning is extremely important as well.

To listen to a lesson at school, children need to be focused for a period of time. This can be challenging for little ones. Children like movement. They need movement! Some children need movement more than others.

In early childhood classrooms, teachers will add in a lot of movement. We have a lot of transitions during the school day for built in movement. Lessons on the rug are usually no longer than 20 minutes, which I have learned over the years is about the maximum amount of time for whole group learning on the rug before I start to lose my audience. Research seems to support that time frame, as most teachers' manuals limit whole group lessons in kindergarten to about 20-25 minutes. To allow built in movement, I will teach a lesson, then we go back to tables for seatwork. Reading groups involve rotating from station to station with rotations being between 15-20 minutes each.

When my older daughter attended kindergarten, our school district was one of the few that still had a half day kindergarten program. Two years later when my younger one started kindergarten, it was the first year of full day kindergarten. My daughter was a "summer birthday child" and among the younger kids. During the first week of school, she came home from school and announced that school was "too long." I felt sad for her. I remember asking if there was any time for play. I knew that research supported play as an important activity for early childhood. I believe full day kindergarten programs should have some time built in for children to move around, exercise and get their energy out. Sometimes we call this "brain breaks."

Full day school is a difficult adjustment for a little child. Focusing for long periods of time is especially challenging. Children need brain breaks. Some children need to stand when working at their tables. That is fine with me. To get your child to focus I suggest some of the exercises I wrote about earlier. Puzzles and memory games will help your child build endurance with focusing. Any quiet activity that requires extended thought will help with that skill. Even drawing a picture and coloring it in can be a quiet focused activity. In this category of quiet, focused activities I would not suggest any device-based activity.

After teaching the full day kindergarten myself for many years now, I now have a different opinion than I once did about the full day program. I now feel that it is necessary during these times for kids to have a safe and secure place to go all day, as many parents are working. I know how to balance the day to make it enjoyable for kids to come to school so that it is not perceived in their little minds as being "too long."

CHAPTER 6

Other Important Skills to Work On (for Kindergarten and Beyond!)

There is a magical word that all parents need to learn to maintain order, peace, and sanity in their own lives as well as the lives of their child's caregivers and teachers. That magical word is, "NO."

Learn to love the word "no." It has such a nice, easy flow to it. Short to say. Easy to spell. It is such an important word to know as a parent! For teachers everywhere I can tell you this word is also a survival tool! You may think I am joking. I am not! If in your past you have been one of those people who has trouble saying "no" to others, I urge you to work on that before you become a parent! Or work on it if you have already become a parent! Learn it now. Do not wait until it is too late. (Think teen years. The teen years are also closer than you think.)

From the time your child is learning to move around and even crawl on their own, the word no should be introduced. Small scale, right away. Use it gently. Use it when needed. Say it softly but firmly. Oh, what a wonderful life it will be for you when your child learns that they do not run the show, that the world does not in fact revolve around them, and that they cannot always get what they want. You may think that sounds dramatic. But I will tell you I have sometimes seen some children (in stores, restaurants, the mall and wherever) who seemed like they were not familiar with the word. I believe it is very difficult for children to learn to follow rules and routines at school if they do not understand the concept of not always being able to do what they want.

In my first couple of years of teaching, classroom management was a challenge, as it is for new teachers generally. You just do not learn that part in college. There was no classroom management course in my education classes. I thought then, as I still do, that there should be a class specifically for classroom management and I hope it is offered now. It was not offered as a course back then.

As a new teacher all those years ago, I was learning on the job in real time what works and what doesn't, what motivates children and what doesn't. Compound that with the fact that I did not yet have children of my own and I really was not used to saying "no" to kids yet! I was really learning on the job. As a teacher, if you have difficulty being able to say "no" and set boundaries, you will not have a sense of control. As a parent, the same goes, in my opinion. Teachers and parents alike need to be firm but gentle. It is a delicate balance and so difficult to master.

Many years ago before I had children of my own, there was a family in my neighborhood and the son was well behaved and well-mannered for his age. He was a very polite, respectful, appropriate child and a good student. One day when I was talking to the mom, I decided to ask her a question because she seemed like a great mom, and I thought she was a good person to get ideas from. While I was speaking with her, I complimented her son's polite behavior. I had just gotten engaged to be married, and I knew that somewhere in the near future I too would be a mom. I asked her jokingly what her recipe was for raising such a polite and well- behaved student. She told me that she believed it was from teaching her children the word "no" from an early age that she was able to guide them to right and wrong. I remember saying, "Wow, that sounds so simple." And she basically said that it is simple, but you must start when children are very little. And I remember she gave an example. When her son was a baby and learning to crawl, she did not want him to crawl into one particular room that had a more slippery floor than the other rooms. When the baby would get to the doorway of that room, she would firmly but gently say, "No." If he kept crawling in that direction, she would pick him up and turn him around, emphasizing, firmly but gently, "No." Just one word. After a few times of being picked up and redirected, the baby learned he could not go in that room and stopped trying. It was simply not allowed. End of story.

When we use the word "no," we need to be consistent, firm, and gentle. Stick to it. I still remember the conversation with that parent and her advice. I took her advice and used it with my own children. It worked well. My children are now teenagers and needless to say, I have had to use the word "no" sometimes. It comes in handy. My advice would be, learn to say it!

In any kindergarten classroom many teachers can tell in the first week of school who are the children who are used to being told "no" and understand it, and who are the children who are probably going to present a challenge if told, "no." Children may not understand why they cannot have their way. Children will ask if they can do a particular thing and a teacher will say, "No, we are not able to do that right now." For example, first thing in the morning, a child asks, "Can we play in the kitchen now?" Maybe that is an afternoon activity. The teacher would have to say no, we are not able to do that now. Some kids look bewildered to be told no. They try to bargain or persuade the teacher that their idea is better. But at some point in kindergarten, children learn the word no is indeed a part of life. There would just be no order in the classroom if each child was allowed to do whatever they want.

If you teach your child the word no, they will be better off for it. You will do them a favor. You will have more peace and control in your own home and life in general. Your children cannot be left to be the boss. That makes for a dynamic that will be difficult, in my opinion. Parents should set the rules, the tone, and the boundaries for what is acceptable, not the other way around. You will be doing your child a huge favor in terms of behavior and character later on if you teach them early that it is okay to not get what you want all the time.

This goes for giving your child too many choices, also. Little brains are not equipped like adult brains to make many decisions. Make a healthy dinner and put it on the table. Please do not ask your child daily at breakfast, lunch, and dinner, "What do you want to eat?" I implore you for your own sanity, do not ask. If you do, you will resolve yourself to a life of macaroni and cheese, chicken nuggets and french fries! If you're lucky it will be pizza! Your child will eat what you eat. Once you start giving choices, you are starting down a slippery slope of appeasing your child. If you make cereal for breakfast, your child will eat it. If your family eats oatmeal for breakfast, your child will eat it. If you like to make rice and beans for dinner and that is your family recipe, your child will eat it. How do I know? I know because the kids don't know any better yet. However, once you introduce the question and the choices, you have an entirely different scenario on your hands. And good luck with that! There is a reason why we have a phrase in kindergarten, "You get what you get and you don't get upset."

I will tell you that I made that mistake with dinner and it took a while to correct. When my children were little, I would ask them what they wanted for dinner. Big mistake! My life turned into an endless reel of spaghetti and mac and cheese for a while. When I would complain, my own wise mother would simply ask, "Why are you giving a choice? Make something for dinner and they will eat it."

Another thing I would stress teaching your child in these years before kindergarten is good hygiene habits. Your child should be learning and practicing good hygiene at home. Children should bathe regularly and have clean clothes daily. If you are running late, there may be a temptation to let your child go to school in pajamas which teachers sometimes see. Try to dress children according to the weather for school, so they are comfortable. A five- year- old cannot know all of the things they need to do yet, so help them pick out outfits. Having said that, I also understand there are children who give their parents a hard time getting dressed in the morning. If you teach your child some independence with getting dressed, allow some choices for choosing outfits, and let your child have some ownership of that process, your child might be more agreeable in the morning. Another tip is having clothes picked out the night before, to avoid last minute stress.

Your child should be learning to brush their own hair and teeth. Of course, supervise these activities until your child has learned the correct way (make sure they aren't running the water and just pretending!) Annual check-ups at the doctor and teeth cleanings at the dentist are routine for children and guidelines for those should be adhered to. In fact, when your child goes to school you will be asked to present evidence in the form of well check-up forms and vaccinations in order for your child to attend school, so please be prepared.

Remember that at school, your child will be using the bathroom independently. Your child should know how to go to the bathroom independently, and to wash and dry hands after. If your child will be wearing clothing that has zippers and buttons (think blue jeans), does your child know how to button up after using the bathroom? These seemingly small problems can cause children to be anxious about using the bathroom at school. Please work on buttoning and zippering before school starts. To avoid buttoning altogether, your child could wear elastic waist.

Inevitably at some point, your child will have a runny nose, cough, or cold at school. We teach the children to cough into their elbows when coughing to avoid spreading germs. Your child should also learn how to blow their own nose, in case tissues are needed at school.

Teaching your child basic safety rules is also important. Your children should know and understand who their trusted adults are, to stay with them, and not talk to those who are not. Teach your child to stay with their trusted adult in public places and not walk away.

Online safety is an issue that your generation of parents now must deal with as well. Many schools have begun digital citizenship and cyber safety curriculums for children. However, unfortunately many children are on devices sometimes earlier than school age and need to be taught at home.

Not every game is safe. I would not allow games with chats and multi players unless you have literally played and vetted the games yourself. Check the ages on apps. Any games that have chats with strangers should be a no. Your children will undoubtedly ask to get the latest games and apps that "all" of their friends have. Do not trust that other parents have done their homework and vetted games. This is an excellent time to use the word, "no" that we spoke about earlier. Your children are going to ask and ask and ask. They are going to wear you down asking for things over time. Feel comfortable in saying no when you know that what you are doing is for your child's own health and safety. Do not miss a trick. Do not be lazy with the supervision of online activities, it could come at a price. Not knowing what your child is doing online is equivalent to letting them walk alone in the street, as far as I am concerned. Do not be naive. Your job is to protect your child. If you must allow it, then limit games. Devices are not babysitters. Always know what your child is doing online. Teach your child to not give out information online.

CHAPTER 7

Following Directions and Having Routines

Following directions is a big deal at school and something that should be worked on at home as well. Small children do well with one direction at a time. Over time you can build up to multi-step directions. Use positive statements that celebrate your child's helpfulness and accomplishments. Show your appreciation when your child listens and follows directions well. That is a good time to use your positive reinforcement phrases as discussed in Chapter 3. For example:

"I like the way you listened and got your jacket!"

"I like the way you listened and put your toys away!"

"I like the way you listened and threw your garbage away all by yourself!"

During the first few weeks of school, I usually give one-step directions. As time goes on and the children become more acclimated to our routines, I add on.

If you hear from your child's teacher that your child is not following directions, it does not necessarily mean trouble with directions for math or reading. It likely means directions such as, "Put your folder in the bin and then come to the rug," or, "Please line up quietly." If a teacher tells you that, it might be a nice way of telling you that your child is just not following rules and procedures well.

When a kindergarten teacher gives general directions to the class, the class will be expected to follow those general and usually simple directions. If your child has difficulty following whole class instructions, the teacher will at that point likely follow up by prompting your child with individual directions. If the teacher notices that a student needs individual, repeated directions on a regular basis, the teacher will likely call the parent to discuss that, because you may need to dig deeper and find out why. If you notice your child has difficulty following directions at home, this would be something to work on.

There could be different reasons why a child is not following directions. Sometimes this is a behavior issue and I would refer you back to the chapter on learning the word "no." There are some children who are used to ignoring their parents' directions at home, and then come to school and ignore the teacher's directions as well. In these cases, it could just be that the child does not respond to authority and the behavior is likely tolerated at home and is a habit. This would be more of a voluntary disregard for directions. I find that positive reinforcement helps and that eventually the child will come around to following the class procedures.

Another reason children may have difficulty following directions is that there could be a language processing issue. Maybe the child does not understand directions? If the teacher suspects this, you will also hear from the teacher with concerns and ideas for next steps.

A child who is not focused on what the teacher is saying could also be missing directions because they are easily distracted by the surroundings. In any case, upon noticing that a child does not follow directions, the teacher will likely try to weed out the reasons and find a "cause." The first step in diagnosing the issue would likely be a conversation with you, the parent.

Then there is the real possibility that your child is just a daydreamer. Some children are. I was a very good student when I was in school but when I was in elementary school, I was shy and a little "in my own world." My third-grade teacher told my mom that I was a day dreamer. She was right! I was looking out the window. I understand and have empathy for the kids who are the dreamers.

Much of school and life is about routines. They say that in our memories we remember the really great moments or the really bad moments. When I think about that in relation to my own life, I agree it seems true. Most of life's moments, or everything in between, we will not remember. Why? Because most days are routine, scheduled days that are very much the same from start to end. That is a reality of life. School is no different. At school we are extremely scheduled. We live by a schedule. Teachers bring their classes to the lunchroom at a certain set time, and must be back at a specified time to pick them up. There is no room for error in that schedule and I had better be there. School runs by periods and learning blocks that are the same from day to day. We have arrival and dismissal at the same time each day and lunch at the same time each day. Children will go to special areas on the same day of each week. It is very regimented- you get the idea.

I will give you an interesting piece of information that I learned from teaching hundreds of children over more than a couple of decades. My observation is that overall, children love routines and schedules. Children love the security of consistency. Believe it or not, it has been my experience that this is true. When a substitute teacher comes in for the day, children have an absolute field day telling the sub the "correct" way to do things in the classroom. They tell the sub that they are doing the calendar wrong, lining up wrong, handing out papers the wrong way, etc. Why do children do this? Because the students are used to their routines and they like their routines. In my experience this is especially true for children who are anxious. Students who are experiencing anxiety love routines, will often ask what we are doing next, and often like to see a visual schedule as a reminder of what is next. If you have a child who demonstrates anxiety, you may notice they often ask what you are doing next or are extremely interested in the schedule. I have found that creating a structured routine and providing a schedule in the classroom helps those children.

A question often asked by many students throughout the day is, "What are we doing next? What are we doing after that?"

In an effort to be proactive (and also to bypass a hundred questions daily), some teachers hang up a schedule in the classroom. The schedule has pictures on it for visual cues so that children can see what comes next. It is on a pocket chart and we can move things around as needed, but we pretty much follow the same schedule from day to day. Again, school is very time regimented and consistent.

Another thing to do is to think out loud to tell the kids what we are doing next. "First, we are going to have our morning meeting, and then we will practice our sounds. After that we will start math." When children know the routine, it puts them at ease. Teachers follow the same schedule most days for this reason.

Children also thrive on routines at home and I believe children *should* have routines at home. At home your child should be used to following some sort of schedule. I am not saying you need to run your home like an army base on a clock. But having some sort of reliable routine is reasonable. I believe a child will become more well-adjusted to have a routine than to have no consistency. Follow a schedule. Do not be over regimented but have some consistent procedures (meal times, bed times, wake up times, nap times, etc.). Having a routine and a schedule at home will help your child when they go to school and must abide by a scheduled day. Do this within reason of course. You do not want to be obsessive over routines. Have a routine, but do not be overscheduled. Balance is so important. Everything is better in moderation!

CHAPTER 8

Character Education

When I began my teaching career 25 years ago, schools had character education programs. Those are not new. Anti-bullying programs were also beginning to become mainstream in the elementary schools at that time. Through the years the programs have changed but it stands that most schools now have some sort of character education curriculum in place. When I say curriculum, I mean that it is probably a school or school district- funded initiative that the teachers and students follow.

It is important for schools to have character education. As a parent and a teacher, I also believe that character education should first be taught in the home. The modeling of good character begins at home with the family. In school we teach character traits such as respect, kindness, responsibility, integrity, and empathy. We encourage children to stay healthy and make safe choices. All of this should also be taught in the home. Hopefully by the time your child gets to school, we are reviewing and reinforcing the good traits- not teaching them for the very first time. The home should be a child's first introduction to the characteristics of good citizenship. The school reinforces.

If families do not teach and model good citizenship and other good values at home, it is likely that whatever a child learns at school will not be as impactful. Please model good characteristics such as sharing, caring, empathy, kindness, and respect at home. Otherwise, whatever your child learns at school may not be taken as seriously and will not have as great of an effect. What kids learn in the school day unravels when they get home if the atmosphere there is dissimilar. We are trying to, as a team, raise good global citizens. Please be the first teacher of good character at home. Please do not expect your child's school curriculum to be the first teacher of good citizenship. Make an effort to learn about the character education program your school is doing, and then try to support it by infusing it into your home.

Elementary school teachers teach reading, writing, math, science, and social studies in addition to all the other smaller subjects that are woven into the curriculum. Character education is one such example of an additional subject. The expectation of the character education program is that teachers and students will model and use the positive language and theories of the program throughout the school day. The idea is for the program to be infused into the culture of the building.

For example, some character education programs have a word of the month or word of the week. School staff and students demonstrate the meaning of the word through their actions. One month the word might be "respect." Next month the word could be "empathy." Or the word of the month could be "sharing." We learn the word and then try to then infuse the word and its meaning through our actions throughout the month. This is just an example of what a character education program might look like. The idea is that over time, your good words and actions become your habits, which then shapes your character.

Each quarter or trimester, teachers write progress reports (report cards) for each child. I will discuss later what a report card for kindergarten might entail. Some report cards contain a comment section for each quarter or trimester. My philosophy is that comments should begin with a positive note about the student's personality. As a parent I loved to see positive comments as well. I will always search for the right words to compliment the good characteristics of a child or good citizenship. I like to point it out when a student has been a caring friend and a good citizen in the classroom because it is important.

You might find it amusing that I am referring to kindergarten kids as citizens. Some parents tell me they love to see that word on the report card. I wholly see these small children as little citizens. The teacher spends four to five hours a day of instructional time with the children every day. In total, we spend more than 6 hours total, minus lunch and special area classes. We spend many hours a day with students and get to know and appreciate their personalities. I do not see the children as five-year olds so much as I see them as little people. Little people, like big people, are capable and can be expected to show respect, kindness, and good character.

Children are so fantastic when they are surrounded by positive vibes and good modeling. They can rise to that occasion. Expect the right thing from your kids and they will likely deliver. Hold your children to a high standard and help them meet their potential. That goes for being a student as well as being a good citizen. We certainly need more of that in this world. Help us get there by raising your children with good, strong values. Start teaching good character when children are young. It will not happen magically later on if you do not build a good foundation.

In kindergarten, try to speak with the children in terms and phrases they can understand. I often told my own children, and my students, that when we come to school or work (children and adults) we have choices. We can help our friends and ourselves to have a good day, or even a great day, by acting with kindness and using nice words. If we choose to say words that are not nice, we can cause someone to have a bad day. Kindergarten children understand that concept and they relate to it. We really hold that power. I try to teach the children to get in the practice of coming into school with the idea that we can all have a good day together. Teamwork and kind words can get us there. When we help our friends have a good day, everyone likes to come to school. I intervene and correct when I see behaviors that do not reflect what we want to reinforce. Parents often tell me their children love coming to school. There is nothing that makes me happier than hearing that. It helps me know I am doing a good job. It is rewarding beyond words. It fulfills my reasons for becoming a teacher.

The atmosphere we create, whether in our homes or our classrooms, is just that. It is created. There are choices made. Words are choices. Reactions to situations are choices. Create that positive atmosphere in your home. At home you can foster that environment as well. Praise kindness.

Regarding character, a good trait that we should be instilling in our children is resilience. There have been countless theories and philosophies about what makes students thrive in the face of adversity, accept challenges, and persevere. Some theories hold water in my opinion, and some are not as good. Over my many years of teaching I have seen and witnessed certain personality traits that commonly go with the high achievers and the kids who seem to persevere and thrive. Regardless of intelligence, I have observed that students can find success by being resilient to setbacks and by having determination. I do believe those characteristics can be really determining and defining factors in a student's success.

Twenty or more years ago, when I taught fourth grade, I often told my students that nothing takes the place of hard work. Intelligence is fantastic to have, but if you are lazy, it may not get you far. It is the effort that gets us where we want to be. Hard work, determination, grit, and resilience are the qualities to work on. Students need to have confidence and believe in themselves and to believe that whatever area they need improvement in can be worked on. Growth and progress can happen. We can learn, grow, improve, or get better at whatever it is that we strive or desire to do.

How do we teach resilience? I think we can teach it by praising our kids when they keep trying hard at something that is difficult. We teach resilience when our kids fall off the bike and we encourage them to get back on and try again. We teach it when we urge them to think about solutions to a problem without solving it for them. We teach it when they lose the race but we encourage them to race again until they win. If your child fails a test, you tell them to study harder next time instead of giving up. You teach it when you sign your children up for a sport that will require practice and hard work, but also rewards. We teach it when we model perseverance in our own lives. All of these are examples of teaching resilience. Success is failure turned upside down. Hard work reaps rewards. These are simple concepts but they have merit.

When we compliment our children, we want to use specific words that enforce the concept of hard work. For example, you do not want to say, "You are so smart!" Rather you could say, "I am so proud of how hard you worked," or, "See what happens when you don't give up?"

We want to embed in our children the idea that the qualities that make them successful are within their control (hard work) as opposed to qualities that are not in their control (intelligence).

CHAPTER 9

Separating from Parent

One of the primary challenges that can happen in the beginning of kindergarten is children having difficulty separating from their parents. Sometimes the separation anxiety comes as a surprise to a parent, who may tell the teacher that their child never cried before. There could be many reasons why a child may cry during the first days of school.

At the incoming kindergarten screening, there are always a handful of children who do not want to separate from parents at the door to be screened. For that reason, teachers sometimes know in advance that certain children will likely have difficulty on the first day of school. If your child is a child who experiences this type of separation difficulty, please know it is not as uncommon as you might think. It is understandable that a student may feel apprehensive when they are not familiar with the people and surroundings of the new school yet. It might be in your best interest to call the school in advance and ask if support staff can be on hand to help coax your child in the door.

As a proactive way of getting children to become comfortable with a new school, many schools will host a kindergarten orientation event, at which your child may be able to meet their teacher, see their classroom, and even meet classmates. If such an event is hosted by your prospective school, please make sure to be available to take your child to it. Your child will feel much more comfortable on the first day of school if they have met their teacher and classmates.

Some children spend a lot of time with parents and grandparents. That is wonderful. My own children did. If you have noticed that your child has difficulty separating from you to stay with babysitters or teachers, there are some things you can do to ease your child into separation.

One of the things you can do is make sure your child is enrolled in a pre-kindergarten program. In many ways the pre-k is practice for kindergarten. It also gives your child practice with separating from you regularly for small time frames. Another action you can take is to sign your child up for some sort of reliable and reputable part-time summer or sports camp. You can usually find camps through your school district or local sports programs. If you are still concerned and expecting a problem at the door, please reach out to the school or teacher before the first day of school so the school can make sure to be prepared to help your child.

Regardless of the amount of preparation, it is inevitable that some children will cry when separating from parents at the doors on the first day of kindergarten. While many children are excited and happy on the first day of kindergarten, the first day is also often a day of tears (sometimes on the part of the parent also). In the next chapter I will address parent feelings on the first day of school.

Getting the children who are crying into the doors of the school on the first day of school is a challenge that occurs each and every first day of school, everywhere, annually. If your child cries, take heart! You are definitely not alone. The kindergarten staff will be expecting it and prepared for it.

On the first day of kindergarten your child's school might have what I like to call, "all hands on deck." In addition to teachers and teacher assistants, schools often utilize psychologists, social workers, and other available support staff at the doors to help with children coming in the door.

Eventually, the children will come in excitedly or at least voluntarily. If your child is struggling with separation, please know it does get better. Many children have a hard time with this in the very beginning of their school careers. It is quite normal. It will get better. It does not mean you have done anything wrong or that you have not prepared correctly. Do not get down on yourself as a parent.

There are many children who cry a little bit in the first few weeks of school. It really could be because of a variety of factors. Parents may be heartbroken, saying goodbye to their little ones at the kindergarten doors, if the children are crying. Parents in this situation sometimes look like they are losing sleep and stressed over their child's crying at school. I tell parents that after they leave, their child is fine.

It is true. Most children cry for a few minutes and then get busy and move on. This is what happens most of the time. While you may be tied up in knots imagining your child crying throughout the whole day, that is typically not the case. Many children cry as they are leaving the parent or guardian, and stop within a few minutes in the door.

I relate to those parents and I know it is difficult for parents to experience that. I will add that over the years, I have seen quite a number of children who cry in kindergarten and go on to be very happy and successful students in school and life. Sometimes they are leaders and run for class office, win sports scholarships, and go on to be honor students. The moral of the story is to keep your perspective if your child is crying in the beginning of kindergarten. It will pass and your child can thrive!

I would advise you to not make unrealistic promises to your child as a means of getting a crying child into the school doors in the morning. I remember a friend of mine once told her daughter that she would wait behind a tree outside the class, as a way to get her daughter in the school door in the morning. Her daughter went in and asked the teacher, "Can I look out the window? My mom said she would wait behind that tree outside." My friend was so embarrassed when the teacher mentioned it later. I can promise you, from my experience, that making these kinds of promises will hurt the situation more than it will help. When your child realizes that you are not behind the tree, there will be a lack of trust.

Similarly, allowing your child to stay home from school or come in late regularly will only delay the inevitable, which is having to come to school. In the long run, those habits will hurt the routines more than they help and may end up being a cycle, making the process harder for all involved.

Every day gets easier as your child grows more accustomed to school. If your child is crying, speak with the teacher for suggestions. Sometimes the children who cry are allowed to bring special toys, pictures of family, draw when they come in, or have special jobs. In a short amount of time your child will grow to know their teacher, make friends, and be excited to come to school every day.

Every year at the end of the school year I marvel, as I remember how the first few weeks of school went. I look back and remember the children who cried during the first week and I am in awe of how much those students have grown. Sometimes those students grow to become the happiest students at school!

CHAPTER 10

Choosing a Pre-K

All pre-k schools are not created equal. As a kindergarten teacher I have found that certain local pre-k programs prepare children for school better than others. I do understand that there are many factors that are considered in choosing a pre-k. Likely when you are choosing a pre-k you will *need* to consider the following factors:

*Neighborhood

*Location and proximity to your home

*Word of mouth (recommended by a family member or friend)

*If your child has friends who will be attending the program

*Transportation

*Cost

*Hours of operation

*Before and after care available on site

*How the hours work out with your schedule

Wow! From that list of variables, it is easy to see how choosing a pre-k can be a difficult task. Kindergarten is rigorous nowadays and adheres to the Common Core Standards of the state in which it is located. With that in mind, if you have room in your long list of considerations for a pre-k, can you add a very important consideration? The factor I am thinking of will be more likely to affect your child's success as a learner than the others: What will my child learn at this pre-k? What programs are offered? Will this pre-k sufficiently prepare my child for kindergarten? In other words, if you would like your child to be prepared for the new rigors of kindergarten curriculum, I think it is in your child's best interest to look for a pre-k with a focus on the following:

*Is there story time? What kind of literature are the teachers reading?

*Are there any formal programs that the teachers follow? This holds the teacher more accountable for teaching the curriculum.

*Do the students learn letters (letter identification)?

*Do the students learn the proper way to hold writing tools? Is proper letter formation/handwriting taught and if so, is there a formal program?

*Is there an emphasis on phonemic awareness (sounds)?

*Is there regular exposure to arts (music, painting), and physical activity (motor centers, outdoor playtime)?

First and foremost, you need to find a pre-k program that works in your life as far as the logistics listed in the first list (needs for a program). If you have the luxury of considering factors beyond that list of needs and non-negotiables, please interview the programs and consider asking about the second list.

Once your child does start pre-k, it is likely that the teacher is a state certified teacher, or may have experience teaching the age group. The teacher may be your child's first formal teacher. Please listen if your child's nursery or pre-k teacher expresses concerns about the child's speech, motor, language development, behavior, or any other concerns.

It has been my observation that it is difficult for parents to hear news about their children that they do not want to hear. I have children and I know that your children are the most important thing in the world to you. Our children are our most precious gifts. With that in mind, it is difficult for teachers to call parents with a concern, when we know that what we are about to say may be the first time the parent is hearing it.

The pre-k teacher may notice concerns and if they do, they will initiate a conversation with you. Teachers, as you may know, are not the professionals who can make diagnoses in such matters. Teachers can tell a parent what they observe and help take appropriate actions, but cannot make diagnoses outside of academics.

Teachers should think carefully about how to approach conversations with the parents in a sensitive way. The first step in intervention is to try to connect with the parent to figure out together the best way to help. Teachers will call you if there any issues they have concerns about. The teacher might list the academic concerns or behaviors she has been observing, and will ask if the parents have noticed anything or have concerns of their own.

At school in these cases the teacher will bring concerns to building staff and begin steps to help the child. At home, parents can be reflective about their conversation with the teacher and call the teacher back if they would like to discuss in more details or if they have any questions about next steps.

If your pre-k teacher calls and shares concerns, please listen and be reflective. Try not to be defensive. We know your child means everything to you. Even if in the moment you are taken off guard and you need to go and reflect on the conversation, that is understandable. Just please do not dismiss the information the teacher is giving you. Please consider and think about what the teacher is telling you. Ask the teacher what you can do at home to help or what the next step is. Whether the issue is speech, attention, behavior or whatever it is, the teacher can point you in the direction of what to do next. Early intervention (early diagnosis of a problem and appropriate treatment) is very important and can make a huge difference if a diagnosis is made early.

Being a teacher myself and knowing that I want what is best for my students, I will add this: I cannot imagine a scenario in which a teacher would take time out of a busy day to call with concerns that are manufactured. In other words, there must be really something there or the teacher would not be calling you. It is at least worth listening to and reflecting on the conversation.

Your first introduction to the big school where your child will attend kindergarten might be in the form of an incoming kindergarten screening test. After you register your child for kindergarten during the winter or spring of your child's pre-k year, you will subsequently get a notification of the incoming kindergarten screening test. Such a test will most likely take place in the spring of your child's pre-k year. Many parents ask me what the screening entails. This screening, which is typically used to place your child in the best setting or class, is probably consistent from school district to school district.

You will make an appointment to bring your child on a school day, probably in the spring before kindergarten, up to the new school. Once there, your child will spend probably about a half hour of "testing." By testing, I mean sitting at a table with a teacher or teachers where your child may be asked to identify letters, numbers, count items, look at vocabulary cards and say the words, use scissors, meet a speech teacher and be asked a few questions, write their name, and maybe take a hearing and vision test if there is a nurse on site. All or any of that could take place and not necessarily in that order! The incoming kindergarten screener may sound intimidating, but is a very basic screener and serves to help the school in placing children into the appropriate kindergarten class for September.

Your child should know their own identifying information such as their first and last name, own address, and a phone number. At the pre-k screening children may be asked if they know their first and last name, birthday, etc. Many kindergarten children do not know the month of their own birthday. You can help your child learn it when you practice the months of the year, and talk about your child's birthday date when the subject arises.

At the time of the screener, you will want to make sure the school has all your paperwork. This includes the child's history (previous schools attended) and information about any services that your child receives (speech, language, occupational therapy, physical therapy, etc.) as this will also be needed in class placement. If your child is to receive any services listed above, your child will likely have an Individualized Education Plan (IEP) that includes how many times a week the child will receive services and what the goals of those services are. Please be ready to share that information with the school so they can be prepared to begin helping your child as soon as school starts, with whatever teachers and resources are needed.

CHAPTER 11

Next Stop: Kindergarten!

After the screening comes pre-k graduation or moving up! Then you will enjoy your summer and sometime at the end of the summer you will probably receive a letter stating who your child's kindergarten teacher will be!

Finding out your child's teacher assignment for kindergarten is very exciting. I remember when I was a kid, we found out our teacher assignments in June. It was folded in a piece of paper alongside our report card and was handed to us in a manila envelope on the last day of school. The memory is so vivid in my mind. The anticipation of finding out the next year's teacher was so exciting. My Mom and I would open the envelope as soon as I came out of school on the last day of school. We would stand on the big green lawn of my old elementary school, a big, red, brick two story building. The last day of school in June, as I remember it, was seemingly always a hot and sunny day. As my mom and I milled around talking to other families, we would ask around to see who else had been assigned the same teacher for September.

Nowadays it seems most school districts wait until August to send out "teacher" letters. In some places, the arrival of the teacher assignment letters is so anticipated that families have been known to avoid making plans to go out on the day those letters are believed to arrive. Families would literally sit home waiting for the mail. One year on the day we knew the letters were arriving, a neighbor of mine found the mailman before he got to her house and asked for her mail early! (No go on that!) But really, the anticipation of finding out who your child's teacher is, in many neighborhoods, an event of much excitement! The letters have become digitally available in recent years. Families no longer need to sit waiting next to the mailbox.

Your teacher assignment letter might come in a thick welcome packet from the school. The welcome packet usually consists of a lot of paperwork, information, and checklists for the parents to ensure your child is properly prepared. There will be information about health forms and vaccinations, and information about a kindergarten orientation or the first day of school. Some schools host a kindergarten orientation or "meet the teacher" before school starts. Other schools do not host an orientation, and your child will see the teacher on the first day of school.

Before school begins, the kindergarten teacher may send a welcome letter and survey. The letter could be general or detail oriented. In any case, please be sure to read the letter. There is a reason the teacher wrote it and it may contain information needed for orientation, a supply list, or dismissal information for the first week of school. Reading the letter and familiarizing yourself with beginning procedures will start your child (and you) on the right foot.

At this time, before school starts, you may feel there is important information your teacher needs to know. Use the contact information the teacher has provided to reach out to her. Things that would be important for the teacher to know might include: if your child has food allergies, an individualized education plan (IEP) for speech or any other reason, if your child is new to English (this may have been discussed at the screener if you attended), or behavioral concerns. Any questions about well check-ups or vaccinations would be for the school's health office, not the teacher. Schools have websites and staff directories where you can find contact information.

Many teachers send home surveys so that you can give some information about your child. Information such as allergies are important and the school nurse should be notified about that also. Do not overwhelm the teacher with other information that is not necessary. If it can wait, and is not something the teacher needs to know, then wait and let the first day arrive. Please use your judgment when sharing information. As a teacher I do not like to begin a school year with preconceived notions about children's behavior. I like to form my own opinion. Children often act differently at school than they do at home. Give your child the benefit of the doubt. If there are extreme behavioral concerns, or if you have something that requires attention immediately, then of course reach out to the teacher. Parents sometimes write on a survey that their child is well behaved, just for the teacher to find out that the child is not. Sometimes parents think their child is not well behaved, and that child behaves fine at school. My point here is that you might want to let the teacher form her own opinion, unless you are sure it is in your child's best interest or there is another compelling reason to tell the teacher at this early time before school starts. Use your judgment.

Prior to kindergarten you will also receive a supply list. The supply list is a list of all the items your child will need for kindergarten. You will bring supplies either to orientation or on the first day of school, depending on what the teacher has asked for.

The best time of year to buy the supplies is after school starts to get a sale for the following year, or the beginning of June when items are fully stocked. A typical kindergarten supply list might have some variation of the following supply list but your child's school will likely send this home when you get your teacher or room assignment, or it may be available on the school website:

Typical Kindergarten Supply List

24 sharpened pencils

2 folders

Pack of index cards (commonly used for sight word flash cards)

1 bottle Elmer's glue

1 box of 24 crayons

1 pack washable markers

1 highlighter

1 composition notebook

1 supply box

1 child's pair of scissors (blunt edge)

1 eraser

1 backpack

1 lunchbox

1 pair headphones if your school uses computers/laptops

Backpack which is large enough to hold a folder and a laptop (yes in some school districts your child may be issued a laptop!)

On the first day of kindergarten, some schools have a cute tradition for parents after they drop their children off. It is called, "Coffee and Kleenex." The parent teacher organization may host this event, knowing that on the first day of kindergarten there are usually more tears from the parents than there are from the students!

The first day of kindergarten is such a milestone day in your child's life (and yours). You want to get your child off to the best start possible. While it is tempting to stay up late and enjoy the last days of summer, you should start trying to get back into some realistic bed times in the week before school begins.

When my kids were little, we started preparing for that first day by moving up bedtime by a little bit each night until school started. Especially on the eve of the first day of school, make sure your child gets a good night's sleep and wakes up with enough time to get ready. It is important for your child to feel prepared on school days. Going to bed on time, eating a good breakfast, and leaving enough time to get ready for school in the morning will give your child some calm and confidence to approach the school day. It will also reduce stress for you, the parent.

As luck will always dictate, expect the unexpected on that first day of school and give your child extra time to get ready. Your child may need longer than usual to get ready, may be nervous, or may be reluctant to smile and pose for pictures! The whole process is prolonged on the first day. You will have supplies to bring, a nametag to apply, and other things will arise. Grandparents may want to accompany you. There may be difficulty parking up at the school as more parents are there on the first day, etc. Have your child eat a nice breakfast, preferably a meal they are used to. The first day of school is not the day to make a stack of pancakes if that is not what your child normally eats, as it could cause stomach ache for an already nervous little stomach. In other words, give your child the best chance to have a successful first day of school!

Be positive and please do not let your child see YOU crying, as much as you may want to cry. Talk about the first day of kindergarten with excitement and happiness, not dread and anxiety. Tell your child, "The first day of school is so exciting and fun!" That will be a much more reassuring statement than, "Ugh! There goes the summer! School is starting!" Even if that is how you really feel, try not to let those negative feelings rub off on your child. Remember you are modeling for your child, and their feelings will be a reflection of your feelings. Our children really absorb all our energy.

Once in the door, kindergarten is your child's first formal step towards a lifelong pursuit of learning. Your child's kindergarten setting should be a comfortable, safe, nurturing place where your child will learn in the optimal environment.

In kindergarten, your child should acquire good work habits and have daily routines. In kindergarten children will learn how to follow directions, share, listen to others, and work cooperatively. If you have prepared your child as mentioned in the earlier chapters, all of that should be no problem for your little one!

A typical day in full day kindergarten could look something like the following schedule. Please note, I am using an example with typical times and activities, but needless to say, times and activities vary from school to school:

9am- Arrival: Students arrive to the classroom at arrival time through their various routes (walker, busser, morning program). Students unpack. In kindergarten, except for the very first few days of school, the children unzip their own backpacks, take out their folders, and put the folders in a basket. They then hang up their backpack, put away lunch boxes and jackets in a cubby, and go to their seat. The children are very independent and can rise to the occasion when given challenges. They are able to do this independently within a few short days of school!

9:15- Morning meeting: Most early childhood education classrooms have a variation of this and it is called morning meeting, circle time, etc. There are different names for what is basically the same concept. Students will gather on the rug for a short meeting in the morning, where we do the calendar, talk about the weather, discuss any fun activities children did at home, and really anything the children want to share. This is also a time when teachers may read a favorite picture book.

9:30: Literacy block usually takes place in the morning. It has been said that morning is the best time for learning. My personal observation agrees with that. Literacy block may consist of a read aloud (shared reading), mini lesson, and in some classrooms, there will be reading group rotations. Reading groups are a time to work on specific skills and strategies, and are usually specific to what a particular group of children needs in terms of learning. For example, one group could be working on letter sounds if there is a need, and another group who has already mastered letter sounds might be working on sounding out words. Yet another group could be beyond that and could be reading pre-decodable or decodable books. Reading groups are a great time for differentiated instruction. Small group instruction is shown to be effective for teaching and learning. I have also found it to be excellent teaching time because a group of five children sitting at a table with the teacher can be more focused and engaged than a group of 22 or so children sitting farther away at tables (whole class instruction). For this reason, many early childhood classrooms utilize small group instruction. When you visit your child's kindergarten classroom for an orientation or meeting, it is worth asking if small group instruction takes place daily. In the next chapters I will describe more in detail the reading skills and strategies your child may work on in kindergarten.

11:30- Lunch: Your child may have a lunch period in kindergarten, just like the big kids! Your child will likely be allowed to either buy lunch or bring lunch. Lunch aides are likely assigned to your class or are available to help the children throughout the lunch period.

School lunches are very nutritious nowadays and effort has been made to make the meals very balanced with the food groups, including fruits and vegetables. If you are pressed for time, school lunches are a good option! Most school districts now offer an online lunch account that you can sign up for and add payments to. Your child will receive an ID number and that card will be used when checking out at the counter in the lunchroom. If you believe you are entitled to free lunch based on income, reach out to your school district, and find out what your child is entitled to. School lunchroom aides, from my observation and experience, are a very kind and supportive group of teacher aides who help the children with buying lunch. These teacher aides make sure everyone has a balanced meal and they watch the children play safely on the playground, making sure children follow school safety rules. They are the unsung heroes of the school!

If your child likes to bring lunch and you will be packing a lunch for your child every day, please read all communication from your child's teacher regarding allergies that children in the class may have. You do not want to pack a lunch containing peanuts if your child is sitting near a child with peanut allergies. If you are unsure, please reach out to your child's teacher. Each school will have different procedures in place for this.

Along with your child's favorite lunch, make sure to pack a drink or water and close containers tightly! We experience frequent leaking of water bottles and containers in kindergarten, which can saturate backpacks and cause major puddles!

You might be apprehensive at first about your child eating lunch at school for the first time. You will soon see that eating lunch at school is a great way for your child to practice social skills, responsibility, and independence. Your child will quickly learn independence as they learn to put the straw in the drink, throw garbage away, and pick out items for the lunch tray.

Recess - Please dress your child accordingly for the weather in case there is outdoor playground time or recess after lunch. That includes wearing coats and hats in the cold. There are many children who resist wearing a coat. I know for a fact there are many children who argue with their parents in the morning about wearing a coat. Teachers try to help the parents as much as we can in this regard by telling the students that if they came in wearing a coat, they must also wear it for outdoor play. The children also soon learn that if they are not dressed appropriately for weather, they might have to stay inside on cold days at recess.

Regarding footwear, if you have a choice, sneakers are preferable and always safer for running around. Children love to run around. While fancy clothes and shoes look nice, they are not comfortable and may lead to slips and falls, of which I have seen many. I might also add that slip on sneakers are age appropriate for children who do not yet know how to tie shoes. Even though teachers tie shoes throughout the day, the laces often come undone (some sneakers even have slippery type fabric shoelaces that come undone very easily) and many trips and falls can be prevented by wearing slip on sneakers. When my own children went to school, they wore slip-on sneakers until they learned to tie shoelaces for that very reason- I had seen enough falls to know!

12:15- Math: In a full day kindergarten there will also likely be a math lesson every day. All the public school districts that I know of use math programs for grades K-5.

1:00- Writing: A writing block might consist of any combination of handwriting, letter formation, journal writing, labeling pictures, word work, learning how to apply sight words in writing, and any other kinder-garten writing activities. Writing usually begins with drawing a picture and labeling, and we scaffold from there. If your child comes in already writing their own name, that is helpful. In kindergarten, as in life, we mainly focus on writing in lowercase letters. Most pre-schools tend to teach uppercase letters first. For this reason, learning lowercase letters in kindergarten is time consuming. Writing is a work in progress throughout the school year, and usually gets off to a slow start as it should. It is very developmental.

1:45- Snack: Please be aware of the teacher's guidelines for snack, and if there are food allergies in the class.

2:00: Some schools may have motor centers or playground time worked in somewhere in the day. Motor centers could include activities such as manipulating molding clay or putty, building with large or small blocks, cutting, and pasting, shoe tying centers, kitchen, memory game with cards, tissue paper crafts, stringing beads, and other fine motor skills. These skills are all very important for building finger and hand strength. In turn, finger and hand strength helps your child in other areas, such as using writing and eating utensils, and in sports etc.

I am in favor of some form of playtime every day for early childhood grades and that includes kindergarten. I believe playtime for children helps development in many ways. Children get exercise and develop their gross and fine motor skills through play. They get fresh air outdoors. Children have a chance to socialize through play. They learn social cues and problem solving in relationships through play. Children use and learn language through play. For some children, the school day is their only opportunity to play with other children. Children learn about friendship here. It gives children with extra energy a chance to release it, which in turn helps them think and focus better back on the classroom. The benefits are plentiful. I have observed this with my own eyes over years of teaching kindergarten. Ask your school if there is time for play in kindergarten.

2:30- Social Studies or Science: Subjects your child might learn about include weather, holidays, plants, animals, energy, etc.

3:00- Dismissal: Children will pack up and be dismissed, either by bus or being picked up by parents. Some schools offer an after-school program for parents who need to pick up later.

If there are any changes in your child's dismissal procedure for the day, you must let the teacher know. That includes changes in who will be picking up your child. Without a note or call, your child will likely be dismissed according to the normal routine. This is because #1- Teachers are not allowed to make dismissal changes without parent consent. #2- Small children cannot relay an important message like that verbally and even if they can, the teacher is still not permitted to make a change without parent consent. For safety reasons, teachers cannot dismiss children to parents' friends, play dates, etc. without a note, email or call to the office from the parent.

At some point during the day your child may also attend what we call "special area classes" such as Music, Gym, Art, Library on a rotating basis. For physical education class your child should wear sneakers. The teacher will give you a schedule so you know what specials occur each day of the week.

CHAPTER 12

Dismissal and Taking the Bus

For some children, taking the school bus is part of the school day. Eligibility for getting a bus usually depends on the distance you live from the school. These distances are often not measured by GPS but rather the quickest way to school using side streets.

When we bought our home, I did not realize that my house was too close to the school to get a school bus. Because of that, I had to reconsider child care resources because I had to change my plan unexpectedly. Because we lived too close to get the bus, my children's arrival and departure status was "walker," which means I had to drop off and pick up my children at school, rather than conveniently standing a few feet away from my house at the school bus stop.

The location of your home in proximity to the school is usually the deciding factor in whether your child will be eligible for the bus. This might not be something you have considered. If you have small children, it is worth considering. What seems like a small detail might wind up being a bigger deal as it pertains to child care, etc. It completely changed my family's work/school/childcare routine, as our daily schedule throughout all of elementary school was shaped by this seemingly small factor.

If your child is eligible for the bus, you will receive information from your school district. You will likely receive a scheduled bus number, a pick up and drop off time, and a bus pass.

Your child's school will likely have scheduled mandated "bus drills" at school. In a bus drill, the teacher takes the class outside to a parked bus, where the children will sit on the bus (but the bus will not move). The bus driver will go over basic bus rules and safety so that every child knows the rules of the bus. This is important for children to learn, even if children are not eligible for or you have declined taking the bus to school. At some time, your child may have a field trip, and for most field trips students are required to take the bus.

You can and should talk to your own child about bus safety before the first day of school, if your child is new to the bus. Please walk your child to the corner where your bus stop is to familiarize your child with the location. It will likely be within a few blocks of your house.

Some standard bus safety precautions you can teach your child include:

At the bus stop...

*Stand away from the actual stopping location of the bus. Do not walk when the bus is in motion. Wait for the bus to stop.

* Walk and wait your turn to load the bus.

* Hold on to the rail as you climb or descend the stairs. The stairs are steep for little legs.

*Before crossing the street, wait for an adult to tell you it is okay.

*Remember that if you cannot see the driver, the driver cannot see you. Make sure the driver knows when you are going to cross in front of the bus.

On the bus:

*Buckle the seat belt.

*Do not eat on the bus.

*Stay in your seat.

*Do not yell on the bus as it can distract the driver.

*Do not throw any objects.

*Do not put hands or any objects out the window.

When you exit the bus:

*Look in all directions and wait for a grown up before crossing the street.

*Stay about 10 giant steps in front of the bus when walking in front of it so the driver can see you.

Make sure your child knows their first and last name, phone number, teacher's name, and bus route number. Make sure that a trusted adult accompanies your child to and from their bus stop. Make sure your child and the driver know who the trusted adult is.

Your child may be nervous in the first few days of taking the bus. This is completely normal! You, the parent, might also be nervous. That is also completely normal! As tempted as you might be to do this, do not follow your child's bus in your car. The driver may be required to report that as a safety concern.

CHAPTER 13

Kindergarten Curriculum: Reading

Core learning standards are set by your state because each state has their own education department. This means that there are standards, or expectations set, as to what each child needs to learn by the end of the school year. Each grade level has their own set of standards to meet, which are in writing and can be found on your state's education department website.

As mentioned, the kindergarten curriculum in the public schools now has a rigorous set of academic demands that children must meet. Some of the reading measures your child may be assessed on in kindergarten include but are not limited to phonological awareness, phonics, high-frequency words, vocabulary, and comprehension (of both literature and informational text). I am not trying to alarm you! Report cards should reflect what is being taught in the classroom in accordance with the state standards. In many school districts the kindergarten report card looks like a college transcript, given the number of measures it includes! Components of early literacy include oral language, understanding of sound structures (phonological awareness), and knowledge of print. Some terms to be familiar with when your child is learning in kindergarten:

Phonemic Awareness - Hears the sounds and can distinguish between them

Phonics – Instruction to help students connect sounds with letters or groups of letters

Fluency- Reads with speed, accuracy, expression

Vocabulary development- Students will learn meanings of words and words within texts. Students will use the words in oral and written language.

In the following pages I will share some of the measures you might find on a typical public school kindergarten report card. Each school's curriculum will vary but for the most part, the following measures are very universal as kindergarten standards go. For each measure I will include a summary of what the measure means, and ideas for how to help your child learn that particular skill.

Under the topic of English Language Arts (commonly referred to as ELA), one of the basic measures of foundational reading skills you will find on a kindergarten report card is, *identifies uppercase and lowercase letters*. This means, is the student able to recognize uppercase/capital letters in a random order?

Accurate recognition of letters is a stepping stone to learning to read. It is one of the most basic foundational skills. Letter naming, as it is called, is an early predictor of reading success. While most reading and writing occurs with lowercase letters, for some reason many of the pre-k classes teach uppercase first. This has long presented a problem in kindergarten, as we really need the lowercase for reading and writing. Your children by this point may be able to identify many if not all the letters of the alphabet, from prior exposure at school and home. If your child does not know the letters, do not fear. The teacher will use a methodical and systematic approach to teaching letters using whatever the school's program is. At home, please reinforce the letters being taught at school.

Letter identification is when your child looks at the letter and can name it. When teaching letter identification, it is important for children to feel some success as a reward. The success builds confidence and will motivate the child to continue learning, so it is very important.

One tried and true way to teach the alphabet is, of course, the alphabet song. Many students arrive at kindergarten knowing the alphabet song. It is very universal. When singing the alphabet song, the children should have visual letters to look at so that a connection is being made. Have your child point to each letter as they are singing the song. Inevitably the "lmnop" part all gets blobbed together! Pointing at each letter as your child says it will help slow down the pace. This is also a good way to practice what we call one-to-one correspondence in math. One-to-one correspondence will be discussed later.

As mentioned, there are many letter puzzles available that you can buy or may be able to borrow from a library. There are some puzzles that match the letter with an animal that starts with the letter. Other puzzles might be an upper and lowercase match. In any case, the objective is that letters are being introduced and presented in a fun way. Your child is being immersed in the letters if you have these types of educational games at home. Kinesthetic (hands on) activities like puzzles really help leave an imprint on a child's learning, especially if the child is a kinesthetic learner.

You can also use flashcards for upper and lowercase letter identification. I would suggest learning a few letters at a time, master those, add a few more, master those, add a few more, master those, and so on.

Another method for teaching the letters is tracing or copying the letters in pencil. In kindergarten we like to also "air draw" letters (make a large motion with your arm in the air, write the letter in the air with just your index finger and no writing utensil).

Another activity to try is the uppercase and lowercase letter match. As mentioned, a fun way to do this is to use a puzzle. But you can also make your own flashcards for matching or play "memory game." Turn 52 flashcards, one of each uppercase and lowercase letter, face down. Try to find the matching uppercase and lowercase letters. If your child is overwhelmed do just a few cards each time you play.

Talk about the visual differences in the letters. Use the child's existing knowledge about letters they have already learned. For example, when we teach lowercase g, we tell the children it starts with a "c." An uppercase R looks like an uppercase P with an added line.

Some letters have straight lines and some are curvy. An S really looks like a snake, which is the same sound that it makes ("ssss"). Examples like this will help your child make connections.

Play games with letters. Find letter cards that spell your child's name. Arrange letters in ABC order. At school we use all the above activities in reading groups and literacy centers.

Another measure you will see on a kindergarten report card is, "knowledge of letter sounds." The letter sounds include all the consonant sounds and the long and short vowel sounds. Is the student able to produce consonant and vowel sounds when shown random letters?

I teach the children that each letter has a name and it also has a job to do. Its job is to make a sound because putting the sounds together can make a word. I try to teach it that way because it seems to resonate more with the children. When testing this, I would simply show a child letters in a random order and see if they can tell me what sound the letter makes. We like to say there are 31 sounds, because we teach the 26 letters but then the vowels each have a long and a short sound. To practice the sounds you can use flashcards.

Consonants are the easiest letters to start with since the consonant letters look and sound very different from one another. But your child's program would possibly start with letter A if the teacher is teaching the letters in chronological order.

When introducing letter sounds, a "picture card" (picture of an object that starts with that letter) is helpful for making associations, as mentioned earlier. For example, if you show the letter A with an apple card, your child will start to make that association of A with the apple and the sound that the A makes. Eventually, your child will move on and be able to "drop" the picture and produce the sound without that visual cue. You can practice saying the letter and its sound and having your child repeat. Repetition and practice are key for learning letters and sounds.

Once your child begins to understand the sound, see if your child can apply the knowledge. Make a list together. Ask your child to come up with words that start with the letter. Here you will really see if your child is able to apply the knowledge about the letter sound. Many times, in the classroom a student will appear to know a letter sound. If the teacher asks, "What sound does b make?" the student knows the answer. But if asked to say a word that starts with b, that requires more critical thinking and some students are not ready yet. The child will be able to do this with more time.

Vowel sounds (a,e,i,o,u) are more difficult to learn and we do spend so much time in kindergarten focusing on vowels. It can be extremely challenging for children to discriminate between vowel sounds. To complicate matters, each vowel also has a long sound and "says its name" in the long sound. When teaching vowels, I emphasize that each vowel has a long sound and a short sound. You can use the same activities to teach the vowel sounds as described above for the consonants. Picture-sound cards and, "Tell me a word that starts with…" are activities you could use.

Another measure you could find on the report card is, *segments individual sounds within a word*. This means, is the student able to separate sounds within a word? For example, can the student say the three sounds of "bat"?

This is a little trickier. Having taught kindergarten for as long as I have, I can tell you that being able to separate the sounds is very developmental. And it may not seem so, but it is complicated. I usually see average ability students begin to understand this about mid-year in kindergarten. Even then, students may not yet be able to isolate the sounds within a word yet. The initial sound (beginning sound) is the first one that children will learn. We start with CVC words, which means consonant-vowel- consonant.

A phoneme is a speech sound. Sometimes you will see the sounds shown in print between slashes. That is how they are often printed in teaching editions. Teaching students to identify the first consonant sound in words is a good place to begin hearing the sounds within a word.

To introduce initial sounds (initial phonemes) you can start by using a picture card, usually a word that has three letters (consonant-vowel-consonant). For example, show a picture of a cat. Say the word together. Then say the first sound together. Do a few of these. After some practice, see if your child can tell you the first sound.

To identify the ending sound of a word (final phoneme) you can use a similar activity. Again, display the picture of the cat. This time when saying the word, stretch out or emphasize the final sound. Have the child say it with you. Tell your child that it ends with a "t." Repeat with different CVC words, (top, hat, sun, etc.). Each time emphasize the end sound. After some practice your child may be able to tell you the last sound.

Isolating sounds is one of the first steps to reading. Please note there may be some time in between when your child can identify the first sound, until when your child can identify the middle or end sound. I have found this to be developmental. Children will always seemingly begin with the first sound. Eventually the middle and end sound will come, and not necessarily in that order. It does take time and please be patient. Each child learns at their own pace.

Isolating middle vowel sounds is very tricky. We spend the entire year of kindergarten focusing on vowels and it is always practice, practice, practice. The short "a" and the short "e" can sound very similar to one another in words and children often have difficulty distinguishing. When shown a vowel in isolation, children can often tell me the correct sound.

Being able to hear and identify the correct vowel *when it is within a CVC word* is a different level and complexity of difficulty. I have found it is best to focus on one vowel at a time, for example maybe teach all the words with a short "a" together (cat, tap, lab, sad, etc.). You can do a word sort, using all words that have the same vowel median sound. Repeated exposure and practice to any skill is key to success. It does take time and progress may seem to move slowly. With repeated exposure, your child will catch on and you will be amazed one day when it begins to click, as I have been amazed and proud each year as students begin to catch on.

Another important measure in kindergarten is, *recognizes rhyming words*. Can the student match words that rhyme and understand which words rhyme?

Many people respond to rhyme even at an early age. Identifying rhymes is an early and basic form of phonological awareness. Rhyming helps children practice the sounds of language.

To help your child learn rhyming, you can read nursery rhymes and reiterate the rhyming words. You can also find many children's books that rhyme. One favorite of mine is, "The Cat in the Hat" by Dr. Seuss. It is very silly, animated, and fun to read with your child. When reading, point out the rhymes or ask your child to find some rhyming words.

Picture sorts can be used to learn to recognize rhymes. For example, find pictures of words that rhyme and have your child say what the word is and find the matching rhyming word. This also teaches vocabulary. For example, a picture card for "sun" and a picture card for "run" would be a match. Supervise and help your child when playing the game. If your child comes up with an incorrect answer and no one is there to correct, then it reinforces playing the game incorrectly or the wrong answer, both of which are counter-productive to learning the skill.

The next level of recognizing rhyme would be *producing* rhyme (your child thinks of their own rhyming words). Being able to produce rhymes usually occurs in succession after the child can identify rhyme.

Practice for this would be to see if the student can produce their own rhyming word, for example, "Tell me a word that rhymes with cat."

Another practice that we do in class is to discriminate rhyming words from non-rhyming words. Say two words and have the child decide if the words rhyme. For example, say, "Cat, hat. Does that rhyme?" In this game, insert some non-rhyming pairs, for example, "Hat, ten. Does that rhyme?"

Most kindergarten report cards will likely also include a measure called, *reads sight words or high frequency words*. Is the student able to read high frequency words, both in isolation and then also in the context of a sentence?

Almost every reading program I have seen in kindergarten includes a list of sight words and/or high frequency words. Those words are often used interchangeably but do not necessarily mean the same thing. High frequency words are words that are commonly found in text for beginning readers. Sight words are words that are recognized easily because of their frequency. In kindergarten the sight words are often on a list of suggested words for children to "study." Even pre-k programs will often have a basic list of sight words for students to learn. Many of the words on the list are difficult to "sound out" because they do not follow common phonetic rules for sounding out. Their spellings are irregular.

Because the spellings of sight words are irregular and could be difficult to sound out, the suggested way of learning such words is to memorize. When teaching sight words, students need repeated and daily practice in reading the words, writing the words, and speaking the words to gain a working knowledge of the words. Some of the words are phonetic and can be sounded out during practice.

The sight words can be taught in the most basic way. The most common method is to introduce the word, then repeatedly model the word in reading and writing, and then just keep practicing. Much like learning letters, practice and repeated exposure is the key to learning sight words. Students can trace the words, and talk about what letters are in the word.

How is it spelled? Trace and repeat. One of the things you can do to have students take ownership of the activity is to write each sight word as they learn it on a flashcard. Have the students do their own writing, and it will give them a sense of ownership of the flashcards.

Also important when learning sight words is to review all the words frequently. We cannot just learn a word and move on the next week because the student can forget the words without practice. We need to continue using the words we learned in practice, reading and writing. There should be cumulative reviews. Review the words with your child regularly at home.

We write the words on index cards and use flash cards daily. I would start with only a few words from the beginning of the list. When your child begins to master a few of the words, add another word, and so on. Presenting too many words at once will set your child up for feeling frustrated. Scaffolding the words is an approach that I find to be more successful with sight words, and for learning letters as well. Learn a few words at a time, and when your child has mastered those words, move on and add more words. As mentioned earlier, and it cannot be stressed enough, it is important for children to feel some success as a reward. The success builds confidence and will motivate the child to continue learning so it is very important.

In my opinion, it is very valuable to give positive reinforcements to reward the learning. In reading groups in the classroom, I give tickets (looks like a yellow carnival ticket) for effort. When students have collected a certain number of tickets they get classroom prizes. This is a great motivator. It gets the children excited for learning and reading groups. I make sure to give the tickets for effort and hard work and not according to "who knows more" or "who is smarter." Again, when we reward the effort, it is a motivation to grow, learn, and work hard to find success. When I reward effort, each child has an equal and fair motivation to work hard and pay attention. You can try this at home.

Following is my own list of high frequency words that I have compiled. In my experience as a kindergarten teacher, these are the words I have seen very frequently in decodable readers and leveled texts. These words are age appropriate to be learned at age 4 or 5 in my opinion.

A

Am

And

Are

For

I

Is

Like

Can

Up

Down

The

We

Be

They

To

Look

Me

Come

With

How

Of

So

From

Go

Say

Said

Ate

Make

By

Do

Little

Big

This

Play

Give

Color words are also important to know. If you ever notice, crayons have the color written on the side. I have been surprised over the years to see how many children can read the color words just from looking at the side of the crayon. They not only learn how to spell the word this way, but also learn the associated color as well. When coloring, encourage your child to look at the side of the crayon to see what color it is. In time they will learn! Red, orange, yellow, green, blue, pink, purple, brown, white, black. Number sight words that are commonly taught are one through ten: one, two, three, four, five, six, seven, eight, nine, ten.

In the classroom many teachers use word walls. A word wall is a display of words. In kindergarten classrooms, the word wall is often a list of sight words that are being learned. Each time a new word is introduced, the new word is added to the word wall. In most word walls that I have seen, each word is listed under the letter it begins with (under the letter A all the words that start with A are listed, under letter B all the words that start with B are listed, etc.) If you see the word wall in your child's classroom, it is because the teacher is likely using it as a reference for students to rely on in their reading and writing. I have had parents tell me that they have made their own versions of a word wall at home. Some use magnets to put the words of the week on the refrigerator.

During the Covid shutdowns I taught kindergarten fully remotely for an entire school year. I saw parents and students being extremely creative in their own homes to enhance their child's learning. People set up mock classrooms with easels and word walls and little desks in their homes. It was nice to see the support and cooperation from the home. Grandparents and parents were getting in on the learning and joining their children on the screen, asking me what page to turn to, etc.

Now that we are back to in-person, at school learning, parents should still have a level of involvement. Children should still have a safe and quiet place in the home that is conducive to learning and doing homework. Having a little desk or a word wall or an easel or a place where your child can play school with their stuffed animals is an excellent idea to get your child motivated to learn. When we learn new letters at school, I tell the children to go home and teach the letter to their stuffed animals or little brothers and sisters. The children love this idea! They come back and tell me stories about the little classrooms they have set up at home with their toys.

A game that can be played with sight words is to place all the flashcards on the table face up. Ask your child to find a sight word that starts with a certain letter. Or you can make it a rhyming game. "Find me a word that rhymes with then." (The answer could be "when").

You can also play a game in which you give a clue about the sight word you are thinking of. For example, if the sight word is "see," you can give the clue, "You do this with your eyes."

Another way to practice sight words is to use the words in sentences. You can do this by having your child think of a sentence that uses the word and say it. If you want to take the practice a step farther, or if your child needs a challenge, you can have your child write the sentences.

Your child's report card may also include a section for *understanding of print concepts* or *reading readiness*. Does the student show knowledge of reading left to right? Does the student realize that there are spaces between words? These are the types of questions that fall into this category.

In reading groups, one of the very first lessons I teach is how to handle books. This includes looking at the front and back cover, holding the book the correct way, learning what the words title, author and illustrator mean and where to find that information. We also learn how to turn the pages one by one. I demonstrate the concept of reading left to right. We discuss the proper and gentle way to handle books and to respect the books as property of the library or the school. As time goes on, some students become very familiar with handling books the proper way and following along. My observation of how the children handle books is one of the ways I assess understanding of print concepts.

At home you can read books with your child to model proper handling of books. I can always tell who reads at home when I see how the children handle books. Children who read often at home are comfortable with handling books and already know the proper way to hold books and turn the pages.

Another measure you may well find on your child's kindergarten progress report is, *decodes CVC words*. Is the student able to sound out a three-letter word that is written in consonant-vowel-consonant form, using a sound-by-sound strategy? For example, "sun."

"Decode" is really another way of saying "read." In my mind it means the child can "solve" the word sound by sound. When students begin learning to decode, the teacher will methodically introduce the CVC words first. CVC words are predictable and are a good way to start to find success more easily. Decoding a word happens sound by sound, starting with the first letter. Remember that learning happens in a scaffolded order. Before learning to decode, students must have basic knowledge of letter sounds. Students must be able to produce the letter sounds before decoding words. See the above section about producing sounds. When decoding a word, the students will say one sound at a time "b-a-t" and then eventually will blend the sounds together. Before the students ever can blend, they will say the sounds one at a time. Blending comes later for many students and I find many students can blend by about January to March of the kindergarten school year.

When we start to decode words is when I really notice which children know their vowels. As mentioned, the vowel sounds are tricky to learn but it is essential for students to have a good mastery of the vowels to be able to decode CVC words. As you can see, there are a lot of moving parts to learning reading!

When I first became a teacher, I became friends with one of the very talented reading teachers in my building. In a discussion about reading in early childhood, she told me something I have never forgotten. She said very simply that to learn reading, students need to know the letters, sounds, and some sight words. In a nutshell, she told me, that is it. The actual process of reading seems more complicated, because it includes comprehension and constructing meaning as well. But for decoding, that is the long and short of it. The commonly known steps to reading include phonemic awareness, phonics, fluency, vocabulary and comprehension.

Once your child can blend sounds and decode, the next step would be to introduce your child to a decodable reader so that your child can practice sounding out words within a text.

Some progress reports might include a measure for *discussions about books*. Is the student able to have a conversation about the text?

One of the things we do during shared or guided reading in kindergarten is to have discussions about the book we are reading. During these discussions the teacher will ask students to talk about what happened in the story, maybe do a retell, talk about the characters, make a prediction, and so on. You can practice this at home. When you read your child a book, engage your child in a conversation about the book. It does not have to be a quiz. Just have a natural discussion so that your child can get used to talking about books.

One important reading measure is, *does the student use multiple strategies to read the story?* In kindergarten, most good readers are already starting to make connections between picture clues, words, and patterns in the story. A lot of beginner books have predictable patterns (the pages all end with the same sentence or there is a rhyming word, etc.)

You can practice this with your child at home. When reading a story that has a predictable pattern, see if your child is picking up on the pattern. You will notice it because your child may show that they know what the next words are before you even read them. Little children love books with predictable patterns and phrases that repeat.

Students may also be measured on whether they can *identify story elements.* Can the student identify the setting, characters, and plot of a story?

The setting is where the story takes place. The characters are the people (or sometimes animals) in the story. The plot is what happens in the story.

When reading aloud at home and enjoying a good book, you can introduce your child to story elements. You can ask your child, "Where does the story happen? Who are the characters in this story? What is happening in the story?"

At school when we read books, we also discuss the author and illustrator and what the job of each of these functions entails. When previewing a book, you can look at the cover of the story with your child and discuss what you think the book might be about (make a prediction). You can point out the title, author, and illustrator. You can explain that the author has the idea for the story and writes the words, and the illustrator draws the pictures. You can use all these words at home when reading with your child. Talking about the books you are reading is a great shared experience with your child and will teach them.

Another skill you can practice at home that may be on a kindergarten progress report is, *retelling stories*. Can the student retell a story in the correct order of events? This is when the child can summarize the story.

Sequencing is a skill learned in reading. Children are asked to recall a story or retell the plot of a story in sequential order. In kindergarten we use a graphic organizer (beginning, middle, end) to help students identify the order of events. This helps students to understand the structure of a story. Stories also often have a problem and solution. These concepts are taught in a simple way in kindergarten.

You can practice this at home after reading a story. Ask your child, "What happens in the beginning of the story? What happens in the middle of the story? What happens at the end of the story? What is the problem in the story? How is the problem solved?"

When your child is reading, watch to see if your child self-corrects errors in reading. It means, does the student reflect on a miscue while reading and correct the error?

Self-correcting happens when a person reads the word, then realizes for whatever reason that they said the wrong word, and then fixes it. When a student self-corrects it shows a level of complex thinking. The little wheels are turning in the child's head. All the moving parts that connect the words on the page with the meaning and the context of the story mesh together and the child decides in real time that the word needs to "make sense," and then self-corrects. When a child self-corrects, it shows understanding of the context of the sentence. For me personally, it is a very cool thing to witness. In reading groups, your child's teacher should and will take notice of whether the child self-corrects.

One measure that will very likely be on any kindergarten report card is, *reading comprehension of text*. Does the student understand what is happening in the story? Comprehension means understanding. Comprehension requires critical thinking, unlike retelling, which is just listing the events of a story and requires memory. Questions that would show me if a child understands the story would usually start with, "Why," rather than a "what." For example, a "why" question might be, "Why did the gingerbread man run away?" Understanding the story and why the characters behave as they do is different from just retelling what happened in the story.

CHAPTER 14

Kindergarten Curriculum: Speaking, Listening, Writing

English Language Arts encompasses more than just reading. Some state standards in education also include the areas of speaking, listening, and writing under the umbrella of English Language Arts.

One measure that is important and may be found on a progress report is whether the student *listens for information.* When the teacher is giving directions or reading a story, is the student able to focus for a few moments and listen?

Sometimes I will teach something, and then a little while later be amazed that so many little brains absorbed it so well. For example, in math one day we were discussing three dimensional shapes and the different characteristics of each one. One of the shapes was a cylinder. I am pretty sure this was the first time many of the children heard that word. I showed them some examples of a cylinder, like a can, a container of wipes, etc. We talked about the attributes of the cylinder, such as 2 flat slides and one round side, what it can do (roll, stack). Then I showed the students some other shapes before I came back to the cylinder. I held up the can again, and asked the children if they could remember what the shape was called. I could not believe how many children remembered it was a cylinder! Those children were listening for information and showing understanding. At home, it is easy to notice if your child listens for information and demonstrates understanding in your daily life. Please know that in school, this is one of the measures your child may be graded on.

One thing your child's teacher will notice is if your student, *uses the correct grammar when speaking*. Does the student use age-appropriate grammar and is the student able to articulate thoughts and ideas clearly?

You may remember in the very beginning of this book I wrote about modeling language for children. Children who have had language modeled for them and have been reading books and literature often seem to have a good grasp of their grammar when speaking. I will give you an example that I often hear at school, "I is going to the nurse's office," instead of, "I am going to the nurse's office." Examples such as that are the common miscues often heard in kindergarten. It takes a little bit of correcting and a lot of modeling. If you notice your child making grammatical miscues at home, gently correct your child by modeling the correct way and having your child say it back to you. If your child is an English Learner (EL), then many of these grammatical errors are appropriate miscues that will get corrected over time as your child becomes more familiar with the English language.

In kindergarten writing, your child's teacher will look to see if your child *uses drawings and words to show ideas*. Can the student draw a picture, for example as a response to reading, and label the picture or write a word?

Before we ever learn to write words, pictures can convey meaning and emotion. This is why psychologists will sometimes ask a child to draw a picture. In kindergarten, we use a scaffolded approach with this as well. We begin by drawing a picture. We later begin to add labels to our pictures in our early writing ("grass," "sun," "sky," etc.) Then later we will write sentences to describe our pictures.

At home your child can practice drawing. Have your child explain their drawing. If your child can form some of the letters, you can help them label their picture. For example, draw a picture of your family and write the names of the family members. Some of my daughters' earliest drawings are pictures of our family with our names written above us. One of them is still hanging on my wall.

As a matter of fact, displaying your child's work is an excellent way to show your child that their work is valuable and you care. When you display your child's artwork or schoolwork, you are letting them know you are proud without even having to say the words.

Also in kindergarten writing, the teacher may look to see if your child uses "kid spell" or developmentally appropriate spelling. This is also called encoding or spelling. It is when students learn to segment words into sounds (phonemes) and make words by writing letters to represent the sounds.

Does your child use knowledge of letter sounds to attempt spelling words? This is encoding, which in many ways is the opposite of decoding (when we read the words). Encoding, like decoding, requires knowledge of the letter sounds. In the kindergarten classroom, we call it tapping out the words. We think of the sounds of the word, one sound at a time, and write them.

You can practice at home by thinking of simple CVC (consonant-vowel-consonant) words and having your child try to spell the words. Again, use a scaffolded approach which builds on prior knowledge to move on to the next step. To have success with this activity, your child first needs to know letter sounds.

In addition to the academic measures on the progress report, you may see some measures for motor skills. The teacher will notice if students are holding writing utensils properly, and this could be on the progress report as well. This is more of a motor skill.

The most commonly accepted pencil grasp is called a tripod grasp. The index finger and thumb are holding the pencil and the pencil falls back on the tip of the middle finger. There are tripod pencil grips that you can buy online or in an education store that will train your child to hold the pencil correctly. Pencil grips can help form good habits early. Using broken, short crayons can also help your child with the grasp, because it forces the child to pinch the crayon.

Strength in the hand and fingers is needed to hold the pencil efficiently. One of the common problems I see in kindergarten is students who do not hold the pencil properly. Students may use too many fingers, the wrong fingers, or even the palm to hold the pencil. The incorrect pencil grip can happen because of poor finger and hand strength, or may just be a habit. Children who do not apply enough pressure to the paper when writing may have handwriting that looks shaky or very light. All these issues can be helped by developing strength in the hands and fingers and with practice to reinforce the correct way.

A fine motor activity is an activity that involves the coordination of small muscles. If your child is demonstrating any of the above weaknesses, simple finger and hand exercises can help your child build finger strength in the muscles to support good writing habits.

To build hand strength, any fine motor activities using small manipulatives that need to be grasped with fingers are helpful. For example, picking up beads, playing with play-dough, making slime, stringing beads on a pipe cleaner or string, or building with small blocks are ways to get these muscles moving.

In kindergarten we do a lot of tissue paper crafts to create 3D artwork. I tell the children to crumble the tissue paper in small pieces with their fingers and then to glue it on the paper. I am always surprised how many children get fatigued easily from crumbling the tissue paper with their fingers, and ask to stop after just a few pieces have been glued. To me this indicates that the child has yet to build good finger strength.

Writing in the classroom also requires children to be able to sit up straight for a little bit of time. To sit up straight, children need to have some core strength (torso). Children who have not developed strength in the core may have difficulty sitting up straight for writing activities. They may also have difficulty sitting up straight when we sit "crisscross applesauce" for story time on the carpet. Many times, children sitting on the rug for just a few minutes will begin to become slumped over, try to lie down, or look like they are uncomfortable. Poor core strength can cause discomfort when a child is sitting on the rug for a period of time. If the child has not developed muscles for sitting up straight, it can be very uncomfortable to sit in that upright position. Children will begin to roll around or will sit in a different position to compensate.

Your child can develop gross motor (large muscle) strength and core strength with simple activities. Rather than play indoors, take your child to the park. Climbing, swinging and monkey bars are all examples of activities that can help build core strength. When coloring, have your child lay flat on their belly to color on a clipboard on the floor. Watch how fast that becomes tiring! This exercise is sure to build core strength! In the classroom during independent reading centers, we use that technique when the children are on the rug.

Have your child help you by assisting when you put away groceries. Carrying items like a container of milk can help your child develop strength in the core. Even holding the door open for someone can help your child build strength. Signing your child up for sports is another great way to get your child moving and develop muscles! Sports also have added health and social benefits for you and your child! You get to meet other parents and children at sports. Yoga and swimming are great sports for gross motor movements as well!

In kindergarten, children will be learning to form letters correctly in their handwriting. As such, this may be a measure on a progress report. Does the student demonstrate proper formation of letters?

The process of writing the letters is more important than it gets credit for. When children are screened for kindergarten, they are asked to write their name. I watch the process as the child forms the letters of their name and, oh my! I see all sorts of strange things going on with the pencil. Letters starting from the bottom, all sorts of awkward letter formations and bad habits are already in place. Had I not watched the child write their name, and had I just seen the name on paper after the fact, I would not have known that the process was incorrect. If I only saw the name in its finished product form, I may not have been able to tell that the letter was written in such a wonky way. But as a kindergarten teacher I do focus on the process of letter formation. We do want children to form the letters correctly. When writing letters, they all begin at the top. There are no letters that begin from the bottom line, which is one of the biggest mistakes I see children making in kindergarten. Many children learn uppercase letters first, and this presents a challenge for kindergarten teachers, as most of the letters we use in reading and writing are lowercase.

There are many different handwriting programs and different school districts use different products, videos, and workbooks to teach the letters. In each program, the focus is on process and formation and there are some standard rules across all the programs. From pencil grip to formation of letters, we focus on the process. When practicing at home, make sure your child is using the correct pencil grip. Tracing letters is a good way to start. You can ask your pre-k teacher for some worksheets and do not forget to start at the top!

On a very small scale in kindergarten, we do have a standard for writing mechanics. We do teach capitalization, punctuation, and spaces between words when we begin sentence writing. At some point in the year, we do look to see if children have very basic knowledge of mechanics and if they are using them in any capacity. Does the student demonstrate knowledge that some words require uppercase and that there are spaces between words in writing? Writing is very developmental and skills vary from child to child. Your child's teacher will be looking at your child's individual progress and growth in writing.

I will say that regarding mechanics, kindergarten teachers teach the mechanics but there are very few children who use writing mechanics properly in kindergarten. We teach it in the hopes that the children who can will begin to incorporate the mechanics. For the rest of the children, we help and remind them as they write.

CHAPTER 15

Kindergarten Curriculum: Math, Social Studies, Science

I n kindergarten, learning of math is more concrete, meaning that math manipulatives (materials) can and should be used to teach many concepts. In my education classes I learned something interesting about the scaffolding of math that I have never forgotten. In early education, the learning of math happens in phases. The first phase is concrete learning, in which the child learns best with hands-on manipulatives and kinesthetic learning. An example would be counting cubes or objects. The second phase is pictorial learning (think of a workbook page with pictures) and then finally children move to more abstract math. In kindergarten, children are mainly still in the concrete and pictorial phase of learning math. Lessons and expectations should reflect that. Practice at home can and should also reflect the stage of development as well. Using objects for counting is a very effective way for children to make concrete connections.

One of the typical kindergarten math standards your child will be expected to meet is to *identify numbers 1-20.*

When shown a number, can the student identify the number?

Children can learn the numbers in a variety of ways. Children need to be immersed in counting and writing the numbers in order, and should learn to recite the numbers in order.

One way you can help your child at home is to make number cards. Number cards, like flash cards, can help your child learn to identify numbers. On an index card, write the number. Under the number, draw dots on the bottom of the card that correspond with the number shown. For example, the card with the number 1 will have one dot on the bottom, the card with the number 2 will have 2 dots on the bottom. When looking at the cards with your child, demonstrate tracing the number with your finger and then have your child do the same. Then count the dots and say the number. You can use these number cards like flash cards. You can also line them up in number order. Mixing them up in a random order will ensure your child really knows each number, even when the numbers are out of order.

You can also use a number line and have students point to the numbers as they are counting. This will give students another association of learning the symbol for the number, along with its name.

Along with identifying the numbers, your child should be expected to learn to write the numbers 1-20 in kindergarten. When the number is dictated, the student will be able to recall what the number looks like and will write it. This is a goal to reach during kindergarten.

There are many children who can point to a number 1 through 20 and tell what the number is. If the same numbers are dictated to a child in a random order, there are many children who can identify numbers, but who are not able to think of what the number looks like and write it. I believe both measures should be looked at in kindergarten, because it gives a more accurate picture of how well the child knows their numbers.

To practice, have your child count the number and then write the number. If your child does not know how to write the number yet, you can write the number and let your child trace. Or, if your child can copy, you can write the number and let your child copy it. In the beginning, your child may write the numbers backward. As your child becomes more familiar with the numbers, you will see an improvement in the number formation. In my experience as a kindergarten teacher, I have most often seen the numbers 3 and 5 written backwards or incorrectly. Your school may have a program that uses certain songs and associations to help when writing the numbers.

Another skill your child should be expected to learn in kindergarten math is to *count to 20 using objects*. Also known as one-to-one correspondence, students can point and count at the same time, or move objects while counting.

Being able to count objects to 20 is a different skill than being able to write the numbers or identify the numbers. A good activity to test understanding of one-to-one correspondence is to line up any small objects such as coins or counters. Have your child count them one by one. This activity seems simple but a surprising number of students have difficulty with this activity and lose count, forget their place, or trail off and forget the next number to say. Some children can count correctly but have difficulty connecting it with the objects.

Practice counting objects up to the number 20. Use 20 pennies, 20 beads, 20 cubes or any other objects you can find. Have your child move the object with a finger while counting. If your child can do this successfully, they have a good grasp of "one to one correspondence." Have your child count the number and then write the number for an additional challenge.

There are many opportunities to use math in daily life at school, at home, and everywhere. In the classroom, I collect the children's folders every morning and as a class we count the folders together up through 25 or so. We also count days of school. I try to work counting into daily lessons in the classroom and show the children real world applications of counting. You can do this at home. Find real life ways to work counting into your activities, thereby teaching your child to count in a natural way. I have found that this kind of rote counting helps children recall the numbers in sequence from memory.

An easy game to play to practice counting is a clapping game. Clap and have your child hold up fingers for how many claps they heard.

You can also ask your child to demonstrate a number with objects. "Show me 5 cubes." Your child will count out the number for you in a group. Repeat the activity using different numbers.

At some point in kindergarten, your child will likely be learning to count to 100 by ones, twos, fives, and tens. I know this seems like a tall order for kindergarten, and it is challenging for many students. Many schools celebrate the 100th day of school and along with that comes a lot of fun opportunities for counting projects, games, and activities. Hopefully your child will have some fun with the learning. Because counting to 100 is tricky, I advise practicing at home to reinforce.

First the students learn to count to 100 by ones, and we start with one. When we count by twos, we start with 2. When we count by fives, we start with 5. When we count by tens, we start with ten. A 100 chart (a chart with the numbers 1-100 with ten numbers in each row) is a good visual for this when learning. Many teachers have a 100 chart in the kindergarten classroom next to the calendar. Teachers use it in the daily morning meetings as we count toward the 100th day of school. Some students may think counting is boring…and let's be honest, for some students, it can be! I tell the students that a good trick for falling asleep at night if they are tired and they cannot sleep is to practice counting as high as you can! Try it, it works! I told my own children this when they were little. Counting at bedtime has two functions in my mind. It helps the child learn to count, and it helps them fall asleep!

Another kindergarten math skill that your child may be expected to reach by the end of the school year is to add and subtract within 5.

Adding and subtracting within 5 is one of the typical standards for kindergarten. It means just that. Later, math facts can be memorized. In kindergarten, I find it best to use manipulatives to draw a real-world connection.

In the classroom teachers use connecting cubes or counters as a concrete way to add and subtract within 5. To do this, you only hand out 5 cubes to add and subtract within 5. I say this because in the classroom, when I hand out the cubes to pairs of children, inevitably a child will say, "You only gave us 5 cubes!" And I tell them, "You only need 5." At home, write math equations one at a time on a small whiteboard (the answer does not go over 5).

For example:

2+3=5

5-4=1

1+2=3

4-2=2

None of the answers, or sums, exceed 5.

Use the connecting cubes or counters to visually and concretely demonstrate the problem. Do this for each problem. Show the answer as written on your whiteboard after solving. Then erase and move on to another problem.

Adding and subtracting within 5 is one of the common learning standards to achieve before the end of kindergarten, so this is a useful and important kindergarten math activity.

To make a real-world connection with adding and subtracting within 5, use simple word problems that you can act out with the cubes. For example, say, "There are 5 birds in a nest. 3 birds fly away. How many birds are left?" Reading has become more and more a part of math, and kindergarten is no exception.

Kindergarten math includes word problems and it will be good to introduce your child to problem solving at a young age as this will surely be taught in the classroom. You can use cubes, counters and other small objects to model addition and subtraction problems for your child like the example above.

In kindergarten math, as well as in science, children will be expected to *classify objects*. Students can put objects into categories, for example, "objects that are red," and, "objects that are not red."

You can teach this with objects of different colors to start with, like toys. Tell your child to put all the toys that are red in one pile, and all the toys that are not red in the other pile. Or you can think of other categories, such as, "objects that are smooth," and, "objects that are not smooth." Classifying objects is a multi-disciplinary skill that is taught in science and math curriculums throughout the years.

One expected math measure you will see in kindergarten is of course, *identifying shapes*. The objective is that students can identify basic shapes. In kindergarten, children may learn about flat shapes and solid shapes. Flat shapes include a circle, square, triangle, rectangle, oval, and hexagon. Solid shapes include a sphere, cone, cube, and cylinder.

You can teach the shapes by using pictures for flat shapes and objects for solid shapes. There are many real-world connections to be made with shapes. Shapes are everywhere. In the classroom we have a lot of fun with this unit. We do an "I spy…" game to find objects in the classroom and name the object's flat or solid shape name.

Another math skill you should expect to see on a kindergarten progress report is *understands patterns*. In kindergarten we learn what are called basic AB patterns as well as more complex patterns, for example AAB, AAB, AAB, etc.

When teaching patterns, one trick I teach students to learn patterns is to "read" the pattern out loud as we are doing the pattern and I model it for them as such when I teach a lesson on patterns.

For example, say aloud, "Circle, square, circle, square, circle, square…" and students fill in the next word, which is "circle." Reading patterns aloud while doing helps us understand the pattern and predict what comes next.

In addition to the standards for ELA and math, children learn basic science and social studies topics in kindergarten. Teaching your child the days of the week and the months of the year, and familiarizing your child with a calendar, is a part of the social studies curriculum and will also help prepare them for life at school. Every classroom I have ever taught in or been in uses the calendar and weather as a morning meeting or start to the day. In pre-kindergarten and kindergarten, we teach songs to learn the days of the week and months of the year. Because of this, many children are already familiar when they enter kindergarten.

As noted earlier in the "typical day in kindergarten" section, science curriculums in kindergarten could also cover topics such as weather, plants and animals, sun, earth, energy, five senses, and other similar topics.

Your school might have a program for social studies in kindergarten or they may do something like a weekly reader type activity once a week that goes with themes throughout the year. Kindergarten classes tend to do a lot of seasonal activities, which often tie into science and social studies themes as well.

Many children come to the classroom full of background knowledge in science or social studies. This is because they have had experiences with their families outside of the classroom. Any time you take your child on a vacation, your child is learning about other places, people, cultures, and landscapes. Your child is learning modes of transportation and about different foods and climates. All those things are learning experiences. If you take your child to a zoo, museum, park, or nature walk, your child is also building knowledge through experiences. Reading informational, non-fiction books can also give students background knowledge in different areas. All these rich experiences, big and small, translate into useful background knowledge for your child!

CHAPTER 16

Interventions, Services, Testing and Data

If at any point before, during or after kindergarten you are concerned about your child's physical, emotional, or social development, the first person you should speak with is your pediatrician. The pediatrician is a good place to start. Your pediatrician can refer you to the correct specialist who has expertise in different areas of concern. Your pediatrician likely has broad knowledge, training, and experience in the areas of child development at each stage. The pediatrician is practiced in hearing the parent concerns and knowing what the next steps are.

Some examples of things parents might be concerned about include a child's attention span, focus, eye contact, ability to work steadily on a project, speech, hearing, and articulation. If you notice a potential problem before kindergarten, please do not wait until kindergarten. Early intervention is key for diagnosing and remediating problems. That is why pediatricians have milestone questionnaires for well check-ups. It is a chance to catch problems early and intervene with therapies.

Just because you notice something, does not necessarily indicate that there is a problem. The issue could be age appropriate. That is why it is important to get advice from a pediatrician who can tell you if the concern is developmentally age appropriate or if there is a need to follow up.

There is help available for pre-school children if you know where to find it. You are not alone. Your pediatrician can point you in the right direction. If your child needs treatment, look into your health insurance and see if the treatment your child needs is covered. At the very least, voice the concern and ask the pediatrician for their opinion. Take a business card for a specialist or get a contact number to bring home with you. Keep things moving in the direction of getting help and do not be stagnant or complacent with it.

Regarding speech, there are many children who may present with what appears to be a speech or articulation problem. Some speech miscues are age appropriate and will self-correct over time. You would need to talk to a professional speech therapist who can guide you. In kindergarten, especially in the beginning of the year, teachers often get notes from parents asking if the child needs speech therapy. The child is entering kindergarten at age 4 or 5 but likely has been speaking since age 18 months to 2 years old. Early intervention is key so the sooner you investigate it, the better for your child.

At school, the teacher and other staff can arrange a screening if needed and the speech teacher will evaluate the child to determine if the child does or does not need speech services. There are some accepted guidelines as to what age children can make certain sounds. For example, certain sounds such as the "r" sound are difficult to make and can be an age-appropriate miscue until about the age of 7 or even 8. Another sound that is commonly difficult for small children to make is the "l" sound. In my experience, these are two very common speech miscues in the kindergarten classroom. Many children replace the "l" sound with a "w." Children may say "wyan" instead of "lion," or "wock" instead of "rock." These are completely age-appropriate miscues in kindergarten.

If legitimate speech or articulation concerns are not addressed by the parent, it is likely the teacher will notice it and then bring it up to the parent. If not addressed properly and treated, speech problems may lead to obstacles to learning. If a speech issue is impeding your child's learning, it becomes an academic issue and at that point the school will address it. In other words, if a child has a speech delay and that is impacting their learning, then the speech delay needs to be diagnosed and treated so that you will see an improvement in academics. This is why early intervention is so important.

Additionally, receiving needed speech services will help your child's confidence. For example, a student who presents with a speech delay or stutter may be uncomfortable about participating in class. Your pediatrician can help you with next steps if you believe your child needs speech therapy. In my observation, speech improvements lead to an increase in confidence in students, which is so great to see!

Along with speech, there are other services that schools offer if your child qualifies. Other services might include occupational therapy or physical therapy. Occupational therapy basically helps people in the areas of physical, sensory, and cognitive problems. Physical therapy is helpful for people who need help in various areas of movement.

To qualify for the above services your child will need a diagnosis. In school, services could be in the form of a pull-out (additional teacher comes and brings the children to another classroom for services) or a push-in (additional teacher comes to the classroom to address the needs).

Other tests may determine need for hearing or vision follow ups. At your child's checkups, your pediatrician will be testing for vision and hearing. At school, tests are sometimes done for hearing and vision as well. Just getting prescription eyeglasses can make a huge difference in learning for a child who needs glasses.

It is important for you to know that you are your own child's best advocate. If you believe there is an issue that is not being addressed, please advocate for your child. The teacher will appreciate you for it. It will make the teacher's job easier in getting services if you are both noticing the same issues and if you are on board with getting the help your child needs.

Acting as a team with your child's teacher and working together will result in the best outcomes for your child.

Throughout the school year your child will probably take a few screening tests. These are usually administered at certain points during the year (for example fall, winter, spring) Screeners are a snapshot of a performance at a point in time and are in no way the only measure your child is being assessed on. Screeners help teachers identify if students are meeting grade level goals.

Your child may also be given diagnostics tests in reading or math, which are used to get data about a student's strength or weakness in a certain skill area.

In modern education we are very data driven. Data drives instruction even in kindergarten. I think most teachers would agree that "kid watch" or teacher observation is also important in the younger grades, as is all the live progress the child makes throughout the year. What teachers see in the classroom for four and half hours a day, 180 days a year, is also a good and true measure of a child's progress and learning. However, data is undeniably helpful sometimes. Having a healthy balance is important to me.

I remember when my daughters were in elementary school, I periodically received results of reading screening tests in the mail. On some screeners and on some days, children may perform better than other times. Sometimes the results may seem off, it was just a bad day, etc. There was always a disclaimer to tell the parents that the screener is only a snapshot of your child as a student. Friends of mine, parents in the neighborhood, would sometimes look at scores, get nervous, and call the school. If you see repeated low scores or the school contacts you about scores, that would be a cause for concern. Your child's real, overall performance through different measures as seen through the teacher's eyes will be shown on the report card. You will also probably have a parent teacher conference for at least the first report card. Go to the parent teacher conference. Do not skip it. It is important and the teacher will tell you how your child is doing in class.

CHAPTER 17

If Your Child is New to English

I f your child is new to English, rest assured. There are many students in our schools who are new to English and/or speak a language other than English at home. If your child is learning English, you may already be familiar with the term ENL, which in the schools means English as a new language. Your student may be referred to as an English Learner, or EL. You should know these terms if your child is going to be receiving services in the school.

Fortunately, and as a necessity, more and more schools are hiring ENL teachers on their faculties. The job of the ENL teacher is to provide support and services for the English Learners. Many children in the schools are new to English and your child is not alone. Many kindergarten programs and school districts have extensive ENL programs now, and this seems to be the norm across all the school districts, from what I see. The ENL teachers are very professional and have wonderful information, training, tools, ideas, and research to support them. English language students are thriving as they learn English and are immersed in the language at school.

The first step to receiving ENL services from your school is a language screening (test). If your child is new to the school, either as a kindergarten student or as a student who is transferring in from another school, your child should receive a new student screening. Before or at the screening you will be given some paperwork to fill out. In the paperwork, please indicate if your child is learning English. The testing will help determine if your child qualifies for the service.

If your child's test results show that they qualify for the ENL services, your child will likely be assigned a "level" of language proficiency. The level will determine what kind of help your child will receive. For example, if your child is emerging and is very new to English, your child may have a small group "pull out" class for ENL services as well as an ENL teacher who pushes in to the classroom to help the teacher for one or more periods a day. The services provided will vary from state to state depending on what is mandated in that state. Throughout your child's time as an ENL student, there should be testing to follow progress and determine future services. As your child moves along in the ENL program, the student will become more and more proficient in English. The goal is for the child to eventually learn English well enough to not need the services anymore.

One of the concerns parents of ENL students may have is that they are worried to miss communications from the school due to a language barrier. While your child is learning and becoming proficient in English, you may not feel that you are proficient enough to communicate. Please know that many schools have interpreters and translation services. Parents of ENL students can request notices translated into their first language. In addition, your school district might have a digital platform that automatically translates the communication into your language if you adjust your settings to do so. Let me give an example. For a parent who speaks Spanish, the teacher writes a message or reminder to the class, "Please send in permission slips for the field trip by Friday." The teacher types the message in English, but you will receive it in Spanish if you have signed up for the platform and adjusted your setting to receive messages in Spanish. More and more school districts are moving to such communication methods.

We used to call it a "phone blast," when we would get a message on the phone from the school district. Now, more commonly these messages are sent digitally to you by email or text. Please sign up for and utilize whatever communication platforms and translation services your school uses. In addition, the teacher, nurse, or other staff members can use a phone translation service when calling you on the phone. We also use interpreters for parent teacher conferences.

Please encourage your child to continue to learn and use their first language at home in addition to English if they choose. Since your child's home communication may be the primary form of communication with family, it is healthy to maintain and build a strong foundation in the native language. I have been told by the ENL teachers that children who have a strong foundation in their first language may even pick up on a new language more easily. Parents can continue to use their most fluent language when communicating with their children.

I always want children to be proud that they can speak more than one language. It is truly a wonderful gift! It is a gift that will help them in life, and, maybe in a job one day. There are many benefits to learning and speaking two languages. How families decide to use their knowledge of languages at home is up to them. Some of my students speak only their first language at home with the family, and in school they speak English. Some families try to use both English and their first language. Some children help their parents learn the language. How each family communicates is different.

Learning a new language takes some time. When children come to school and they are new to a language, they are first learning about their surroundings, learning social cues, and maybe even learning about a new culture. These children may be quiet in school in the beginning as they take in all the new information. So, if your child seems shy or quiet in the beginning of school, please know that this is normal.

Some students have just moved here from another country right before school began. Their families do not speak English. Some children may cry the first few days of school, and parents might worry. We assure parents that their child will be okay. We hold the children's hands coming into school if they are scared for the first time in a new place. Each day the children learn, make friends, play, begin to laugh and become more comfortable. It is so amazing and wonderful to watch and be a part of.

Three months later at a parent teacher conference, parents often thank the teachers and tell us that that their child loves school so much and they are sad on days off! Children are very resilient by nature, and they also absorb new information easily.

Rest assured English learners will be held to the same standards of learning and teachers will hold high expectations for all students. Teachers may use visual cues, a buddy system, and other strategies to help your child as they assimilate into the English language. When you speak with your child's teacher, feel free to ask the teacher what ENL tools or strategies are being used in class.

If your child is new to English and you have been concerned about that, I hope that this information has eased your worries. I also encourage you to reach out to your school's ENL coordinator or teacher to find out information before school starts. Translation services for phone calls should be available for you when you call.

CHAPTER 18

The Importance of the Home School Connection

I want parents to know that it is essential to work as a team with your child's teacher to help your child achieve success. Both parent and teacher can each do their separate jobs with good results, but when we work together it is better for the child and can achieve a common goal.

The parent-teacher relationship is a unique one. Parents entrust their most precious gift in their life to us. I realize the importance of that. No question is silly. Parents' feelings are real, as are children's feelings. It is hard to not think with your heart when you are a parent. It is sometimes difficult to not let emotions get in the way if you are annoyed about something that happened at school. Your child did not eat their lunch, for example, and you are worried. Reach out to the teacher and express your concerns. There may be a reasonable explanation why your child is not eating lunch. Maybe your child is talking and making friends. Sometimes there is a simple and easy solution.

In kindergarten, parents call or email all the time. They sometimes apologize and preface the conversation with, "This probably sounds ridiculous but..."

I was a new parent of a kindergartener once too. I know all the emotions of sending your child to the big school for the first time, a long day away from home it seems. I do not think any question is silly. When in doubt, always ask the teacher.

It is very important to maintain regular communication with your child's kindergarten teacher and to have a home school connection. It also sets the scene for you to become involved in your child's school life going forward. Keep the teacher in the loop if there are changes in the home, if you are moving houses or apartments, if a divorce is going on, if there is a new baby at home, etc. When milestone events happen in a child's life, sometimes we see behavioral changes. At the very least a child may seem out of sorts at school. Let the teachers know so we can give some extra attention to your child as they go through a difficult or new event in their life.

Teachers communicate with parents through calls, notes, or emails-any of the above really. When you have a concern and are about to reach out to your child's teacher, please do so politely. A wise expression states that, "You can catch more flies with honey." I am a parent too and I understand that when we are feeling upset or concerned, our emotions can get in the way and messages can be conveyed in a less than professional way. As a parent, I was that person at times to initiate calls to my own children's teachers to get clarity on something or express a frustration about how something was handled at school. I always tried to remember that cooler heads prevail and tried to take a step back to cool off before I made the call.

On the other side of that, I have been teaching a long time and I no longer take offense when parents sound upset on the phone, for whatever the reason may be. Parents can be upset for a range of reasons, even down to the child not eating their whole snack. Just remember that for optimal results, it is in your best interest to express yourself in a professional and respectful way when dealing with any adult, and that includes your child's teacher. Your child's teacher should reciprocate the respect.

School districts also now have new digital communication platforms that are used district wide. Please sign up for any communication platforms your school district sends out. If you do not, you will miss out on important phone blasts for things like school closings, days off, schedule changes, fundraisers, school events, parent teacher night, parent organizations or board meetings, and so many other things.

It is super important to be involved on some level in your child's education. That means reinforcing what is taught at school, as well as showing the teacher and the school that the family is involved. Families should be at least somewhat involved in their child's education. Your communication and involvement are sending an impression to the teacher that you care.

I find that children from homes of families that are involved in their educational life and school just seem overall more confident and assured. It speaks volumes to a child if you are interested in their school day. Learn your children's teachers' names, and ask them about their school day.

In regards to attending events at your child's school, at the very least is what I would call basic involvement. At this level of involvement, parents or guardians attend what I believe are the important school events- the ones I feel are very essential to attend. These events include the orientation, the parent teacher conference, any meetings regarding school services your child will be receiving, and end of year graduations or ceremonies. Regardless of work schedule and other obligations, please try to attend some of your child's events. Your child's schooling and education is an important obligation and responsibility as well. If a parent or guardian skips important events at school, it may be because there are other obligations. Please reach out to the teacher if you are finding you cannot attend events, and maybe the teacher can work with your schedule.

If you have time, in addition to attending the above-mentioned events (orientation, parent teacher conference, any meetings regarding school services your child will be receiving, and end of year graduations) you may also pay a small fee to have a membership in your school's parent organization and may volunteer to attend a few extra events per year (class parties, field day, trips, fundraisers).

Some parents have additional time to spare or desire to be involved at an even higher level. That includes parents/guardians who attend most events, sign up to be a class parent or active volunteers in school events, volunteer to chair events, etc.

If possible, try to volunteer at some school events like book fairs or carnivals or class parties. Attend class picnics, shows, graduations, and everything you can.

Childhood goes very fast. My own children were in high school and college before I knew it, and I do not know where the years went! When my kids were little, I was as involved as my schedule would allow and I did all the extra events I could. At the end of the work day, I would say to my friend, another teacher, "Now I am going to coach my daughter's team, I am exhausted." And my very wise friend at work, who had older kids, would tell me, "You'll never look back and wish you did less." That was her expression. It is so true. It became my mantra when I was tired from work and parenting. It became my personal rally cry. I repeated it to other parents who were tired also. I look back and I am so grateful I did everything I could possibly do for my kids when they were little. In the final analysis, it is all about the love you give. You will not regret it if you are present for your children, no matter how tiring it may be or what a sacrifice it might seem like in the moment. The days go slow but the years go fast. You may, however, regret it if you do not do what you can now. You will never get that time back. So be as involved as possible. Your children will likely be healthier emotionally and have more self-esteem, because your involvement shows your children you value them and love them. You can find a balance between working and helping at your child's school. I see many working parents who do it. Many of the parents who help at school and attend events also work full time. Working and being involved at your child's school are not mutually exclusive.

If you do not know where to start, the above-mentioned parent organization is a great place to start. It may be called PTA or PTO at your school, but the idea is the same. Parent associations run so many wonderful programs for the kids. They host book fairs, holiday boutiques, school stores, carnivals, dances, fundraisers, healthy snack days, auctions, and a lot of other fun events.

I once was at a friend's baby shower. At the table was a friend whose daughter had just started kindergarten. She told a story about back-to-school night at her daughter's school. When a volunteer at the parent organization booth asked her if she and her husband would like to get a membership, she said she ran away down the hall! She was scared she would be asked to do lots of stuff! She said she did not join because she was afraid they were going to ask her to do lots of things that she did not have time for. The other moms and I at the table assured her that is not true. Your membership money likely goes to all the events and fun things the organization plans for school, which can include book fairs, carnivals, fundraisers, field trips, etc. Just because you have a membership does not mean you need to volunteer your time or attend meetings. However, if you do volunteer in any small way, your child will love it because they may see you at school.

There might also be an opportunity to be a class parent or a parent helper. Teachers understand that class parents are busy too. The class parent job often involves communication with the parents, and helping to organize class parties and events. Class parents are usually chosen at the start of the school year so if you are interested, reach out to your child's teacher. As a teacher, it is always my hope that each parent will have a chance to help at some point during the year, because the children absolutely love it when their parents come to school!

As an aside I will strongly suggest that while being involved in your child's school, you should make sure to follow the school's guidelines and policies for events. Rules are for safety. Sadly, but for necessity, over the past ten years or so all schools have begun to require identification for sign in. This includes grandparents or anyone else who might be attending your child's school event. Please do not be offended if you or any family members or grandparents are asked for identification to attend an event at your child's school. Please know this is for the safety of your own child and everyone in the school building. The security guards or monitors at the door do not have time to haggle with visitors about identification. If you forgot it, you may be asked to go home and get it. We often send reminders before events about bringing identification.

Please adhere to the school's safety rules and requests so that events can be safe and enjoyable for all. Please follow rules and guidelines for events, which will likely be sent in advance of events (number of guests, where to park, etc.) When in doubt about guidelines for an event, please ask the teacher.

On the topic of attending your child's school events: This should go without saying but if you or a family member has told a child that you will attend a school event, please make sure you show up. I have seen little tears that have broken my heart over the years when a child was expecting a parent who did not show. We all know that things come up. Please find a family member to take your place or notify the teacher so the teacher can be prepared and come up with something to do, like asking a special area teacher to fill in. When teachers have a little time to find a solution, we usually can. We are resourceful and think quickly. It is not so easy when we have no warning.

I am reminded of an event one school used to host some years ago. Parents were able to sign up to be a "mystery reader" for the kindergarten class. There was a schedule, and every Friday a different parent or family member was allowed to come in and read to the class. The class did not know until the reader arrived who it would be, hence the "mystery." Occasionally the parent who was assigned to come did not come. Something had come up or they forgot. When something like that happens, the child and the class are disappointed and the teacher needs to think quickly to smooth it over.

Schools are very time oriented so please be respectful of that. If a parent teacher conference, school play, or book sale is set to begin at a certain time, please be there on time as these events cannot wait for parents who are running late. In addition, your child will be disappointed if every other child's parent has arrived and your child is still waiting.

Please make sure to follow school policies in regards to food as well. Food is a big one. Many children have various food allergies. Every year there are children with food allergies in every school, everywhere. Every year many letters go home with guidelines about what can and cannot be sent in for lunch, snack, and birthdays. Not following the food guidelines causes a safety issue as well as hurt feelings. Please be mindful of all the notices that are sent home. If that was your child who had a food allergy, you would wish for other parents to be respectful of your child's food allergy. Please treat others in kind.

The teacher will send notices in the folder or there will be reminders on the school communication platform. Please read any and all communication from your child's school to stay in the loop.

CHAPTER 19

Homework in Kindergarten (?!)

When I taught fourth grade, there was a known rule of thumb about homework that many teachers followed. This guideline indicated that in first grade teachers should assign 10 minutes of homework, in second grade teachers should assign 20 minutes of homework, 30 minutes for third grade, 40 minutes for fourth grade, 50 minutes for fifth grade and so on.

Some years into my teaching career, I changed grades and moved to kindergarten. I thought about the guideline I had been following and wondered where kindergarten fit into that. I decided on a different philosophy for kindergarten homework. My philosophy was that kindergarten homework would be a very simple reinforcement of some skill that had been taught at school, or maybe reading a book with an adult, or studying sight words or any combination of those things. But most importantly to me, it should be a meaningful reinforcement and should be short because I want kids to have time for play, which is lessened with the full day kindergarten. I felt validated in my philosophy when my own children went to kindergarten and needed that balance. I felt that my decision on homework was the right thing for the children.

I am not big on giving a lot of homework worksheets in kindergarten because I think organic activities like playing outside, exercise and exploratory play are more important for early childhood age children. I believe homework in kindergarten should be a practice for getting homework in the later grades. It is about getting used to doing homework and the routine that it represents. To me, it is more about learning the routines of being a student and the expectations and responsibilities that go along with that, more than it is doing a lot of busy work. I do not like busy work that has no meaningful lesson. I believe in meaningful school work that has purpose.

Homework is a reinforcement of lessons or activities done in school. Most of the time it will be a simple reading, math, writing, or fine motor activity, which the child should be able to complete with little or no assistance.

Please be actively engaged in your child's homework activity, as this will help your child understand the importance of homework. Your child should write his or her name on the homework. At the beginning of the year, the first name is fine. If your child is not yet writing independently, please write the name lightly and have your child trace over your writing. All writing for homework should be done in pencil. In the first week of school, students sometimes hand in homework that has been written in crayon. Each teacher may have different expectations.

Reading to and with your child is very important and should be part of your daily routine. I encourage you to read with your child each day. If you do not have many books at home, I encourage you to go to your public library. The selection is impressive and the children can find all their favorites there! Do not be surprised if your child wants to read the same book repeatedly. Children enjoy the familiarity and repetition of books they know and a great story can be enjoyed time and time again!

Your child might use a homework folder. I think every teacher I know has the children set aside a folder for homework and back-and-forth communications with home. In my class, the homework folder is still a major method of communication. While many schools have online forms of parent communication, the folder is still a mainstay as some families are not signed up for digital communications.

In my classroom, a homework sheet is placed in the folder and is completed by the student and returned the next day. All notices, reminders, and homework assignments go home in the folder. Likewise, we ask parents that notes, change in dismissal notices, envelopes with money, and any other important things coming to school go in the folder. You should check your child's folder every day if your child is in kindergarten. When I see folders that have not been viewed or cleaned by parents, I send reminders. The back-and-forth communication through the folder helps ensure the child's success in school at this young age.

If families speak another language other than English, we can translate the communications. Again, please sign up for any electronic communications your school district uses that might have automatic interpretation. Letters and communications home to parents can be translated easily on some platforms. Schools may offer tutoring services, extra help or after school programs that can help with homework. If your child needs help with homework and you are having difficulty helping them because of a language barrier, ask what services are in place to help you. Lessons will be the same and there is support for English language learners.

CHAPTER 20

A Kindergarten Teacher's
Favorite Books for Read Alouds

The poem "Invitation" by Shel Silverstein is one of my favorite poems and in a way, brings me back to the reasons I became a teacher in the first place. In my very first classroom I made a poster and hand wrote that poem on it and hung it on my classroom door. The poem summed up how I wanted children to feel when they came to school. I wanted them to be filled with wonder, imagination, excitement, and a wish to learn more and more. I wanted it to be a space inclusive and safe for all. The poem to me means all of that and more.

I have a very specific memory of the librarian in the grade school I attended as a child. I remember sitting on the carpet listening intently to her, as she read a book aloud to the class each week. I remember trying to find a spot on the rug where I could see the pictures without craning my neck. I remember searching the shelves looking for the perfect book to borrow, hoping I would find it before the bell rang. I am not sure, but I wonder if that was where my love of reading began. It is certainly one of my earliest memories of loving books. I hope for my students to also fall in love with books.

Watching the expressions of wonder and amusement on children's faces upon reading a good book has been one of the greatest joys and gifts of my life as a Mom, and as a teacher. It continues to be a gift each day. I love the look on children's faces and the sound of laughter when we read a great book. I love the organic discussion that happens through the events in the stories and the excitement children have when they make a text-to-self connection.

Children love read alouds. There are so many great stories out there for young readers! I am talking about picture books with so much imagination and beautiful pictures, as well as big laughs and silliness, and sweet stories about friendship and kindness. Please do not miss these years of reading to your child and with your child. You cannot get these years back.

Picture books have endless learning opportunities. As you are reading books with your child, remember to have conversations about the books. This will help your child grow in language, vocabulary, and conversation. The pictures bring the story to life. As you are reading, discuss the characters, the setting, and the plot. Make a prediction about what might happen next. Talk about whether you liked the ending. Figure out the problem and solution in the book. Stopping and thinking about the book is what good readers do. Modeling that will help your child become a thoughtful reader. The learning part happens naturally. It does not need to feel forced or as if you are quizzing your child. You want the teaching and learning to happen in the natural flow of the conversation about the book. Reading should be an enjoyable experience for children.

You will be absolutely amazed how much your child will begin to love reading if you find great books.

I have a seemingly endless list of favorite stories, and gosh I have read so many throughout the years. I know which parts are the happy parts, the sad parts, the scary parts (I am envisioning the look on faces when the gingerbread man gets eaten! We hate that part! So, we write our own ending in class!)

I would love to share with you my favorite "tried and true" kindergarten read aloud recommendations (popular with my classes year after year as well as with my own children when they were little). Many of these titles can be found in your local public library. Borrow books for free and return them by the due date and you will have an endless reading supply. My hope is for you to share these wonderful stories with your little learners so that they grow to love good stories as well. This is one of the best and easiest educational gifts you can give to your child. As we say in kindergarten, "Happy reading!"

Fun, Educational

Chicka Chicka Boom Boom by Bill Martin Jr.

Diary of a Worm by Doreen Cronin

From Head to Toe by Eric Carle

One Tiny Turtle by Nicola Davies

Chase the Moon Tiny Turtle by Kelly Jordan

From Seed to Plant by Gale Gibbons

Penguins, Penguins Everywhere by Bob Barner

Lucky Ducklings (A True Rescue Story) by Eva Moore

Sweet Stories about the Rewards of Hard Work/Learning

Rocket Learns to Read by Tad Hill

Rocket Learns to Write by Tad Hill

The Art Lesson by Tomie dePaola

The Little Engine that Could by Watty Piper

Leo the Late Bloomer by Robert Kraus

Giraffes Can't Dance by Giles Andrede

Imagination

Goodnight Gorilla by Peggy Rathmann

Sylvester and the Magic Pebble by William Steig

Harold and the Purple Crayon by Crockett Johnson

The Mitten by Jan Brett

Where the Wild Things Are by Maurice Sendak

The Salamander Room by Anne Mazer

Love/ Separation

The Kissing Hand by Audrey Penn

Knufflebunny by Mo Willems

Knufflebunny Too by Mo Willems

Knufflebunny Free by Mo Willems

Alexander and the Wind Up Mouse by Leo Leonni

Corduroy by Don Freeman

Love You Forever by Robert Munsch

Big Laughs

The Day the Crayons Quit by Drew Daywalt

No David by David Shannon

David Goes to School by David Shannon

Five Little Monkeys by Eileen Christelow

The Book with No Pictures by B.J. Novak

Skippyjon Jones Class Action by Judy Scheckner

Seasonal/ Weather

I am the Wind by Michael Karg

Snowmen at Night by Caralyn Buehner

A Story for Bear by Dennis Haseley and Jim LaMarche

The Luckiest Snowball by Elliot Kreloff

Good-bye, Winter! Hello, Spring! By Kazuo Iwamura

The Apple Pie Tree by Zoe Hall

Sharing/Kindness

Rainbow Fish by Marcus Pfister

Mr. Peabody's Apples by Madonna

The Giving Tree by Shel Silverstein

How Full is Your Bucket? For Kids by Tom Rath and Mary Reckmeyer

Fill a Bucket (Guide to Happiness) by Carol McCloud

Corduroy by Don Freeman

Honesty

Betty Bunny Didn't Do It by Michael Kaplan

My Favorite Authors

Peter's Chair by Ezra Jack Keats

Whistle for Willie by Ezra Jack Keats

Apt 3 by Ezra Jack Keats

The Snowy Day by Ezra Jack Keats

Wemberly Worried by Kevin Henkes

Kitten's First Full Moon by Kevin Henkes

Sheila Rae, the Brave by Kevin Henkes

Lilly's Big Day by Kevin Henkes

Chrysanthemum by Kevin Henkes

Favorite Characters

Pete the Cat series by James Dean

Ladybug Girl by David Somers and Jacky Davis

Ladybug Girl and Bumblebee Boy by David Somers and Jacky Davis

Ladybug Girl at the Beach by David Somers and Jacky Davis

Ladybug Girl at the Bug Squad by David Somers and Jacky Davis

Clifford the Big Red Dog series by Norman Bridwell

Froggy series by Jonathan London

My Favorite Book Series

Curious George by H.A. Rey

Pinkalicious Series (Pinkalicious, Silverlicious, Purplicious) by Victoria Kann

How Do Dinosaurs…. By Jane Yolen and Mark Teague

Froggy series books by Jonathan London

Llama Llama series by Anna Dewdney

Understanding Disabilities

Angel and her Wonderful Wheels: A True Story of a Little Goat Who Walked with Wheels by Leanne Lauricella